Children's Illustrated
HISTORY ATLAS

Authors Simon Adams, Peter Chrisp
Senior editor Lizzie Davey
Project art editor Hoa Luc

Map illustrator Jeongeun Park
Cartography Ed Merritt
Illustrator Molly Lattin
Editorial Abhijit Dutta, Satu Fox,
Roohi Sehgal, Kathleen Teece, Amina Youssef
Design Yamini Panwar, Nehal Verma
Picture researcher Sumita Khatwani
Jacket co-ordinator Francesca Young
Jacket designer Suzena Sengupta
Managing editor Laura Gilbert
Managing art editor Diane Peyton Jones
Pre-production producer Dragana Puvacic
Producer Basia Ossowska
Design director Helen Senior
Publishing director Sarah Larter

First published in Great Britain in 2018 by
Dorling Kindersley Limited
80 Strand, London, WC2R 0RL

Copyright © 2018 Dorling Kindersley Limited.
A Penguin Random House Company
10 9 8 7 6 5 4 3 2 1
001-308500-Aug/2018

A CIP catalogue record for this book
is available from the British Library

ISBN: 978-0-2413-1990-1

Printed and bound in Malaysia

A WORLD OF IDEAS:
SEE ALL THERE IS TO KNOW

www.dk.com

Contents

4 How to use this book
6 World people

8 The Ancient World
10 Timeline of the Ancient World
12 The Stone Age
14 Mesopotamia
15 The Indus Valley
16 Ancient Egypt
18 Ancient Greece
20 Ancient China
22 Ancient Rome
24 Religion

26 The Middle Ages
28 Timeline of the Middle Ages
30 The Vikings
32 Ancient Japan
33 Ancient Korea
34 Indigenous people of
North America

36 African empires

38 The Silk Road

40 The Middle Ages

42 The Age of Discovery

44 Timeline of the Age of Discovery

46 Aztec and Maya civilizations

47 The Inca Empire

48 Voyages of discovery

50 The Mughal Empire

52 The Ottoman Empire

54 The Renaissance

56 The Slave Trade

58 The Age of Industry

60 Timeline of the Age of Industry

62 The US Revolution

63 The French Revolution

64 The Industrial Revolution

66 The US Civil War

68 Imperial world

70 The Modern World

72 Timeline of the Modern World

74 Inventions

76 World War I

78 New ideas

80 World War II

82 Independent world

84 The Cold War

86 The Space Age

88 The world today

90 Picture quiz

92 Glossary

93 Index

96 Credits

How to use this book

A map is a drawing that gives an overall view of a place. The maps in this book show parts of the world at different times in history. These are often very different to how the same areas are split into countries today.

Outside areas
Around the edges of many of the maps are other land areas. These are shown in a cream colour.

Dates
On the map, dates are shown in bold, to help you find your way around the page.

Picture features
Pictures with text pick out special features, including buildings and battles.

Important cities
Capital cities are marked with red outlines. Other cities are outlined in blue.

Ancient Rome

More than 2,000 years ago, Ancient Rome was one of the most powerful nations in the world. At first, Rome was ruled by kings. It became a republic in 509 BCE, which meant that it was ruled by members of Roman society. In 27 BCE Rome became an empire, led by a ruler called an emperor. At its largest, in 117 CE, the Roman Empire was home to more than 65 million people.

Snapshots
These images add extra information about historical events, people, and places.

Key
The key lists important features that link to the picture symbols on the map.

Date
Some of the keys have a date to show the time period of the map. If the date includes "c." it means "circa", or "around" — which means that the date isn't exact.

Compass
The compass always points to north (N) on the map and also shows the direction of south (S), east (E), and west (W).

Punic Wars
Between 264 and 146 BCE, Rome fought three wars against the city of Carthage in modern-day Tunisia. They wanted control of the Mediterranean Sea. The wars, known as the Punic Wars, ended in total Roman victory.

General Hannibal from Carthage

KEY (c. 117 CE)

Empire border
The edge of the Roman empire.

Grain
Shipped to Rome from North Africa and Sicily.

Grapevines
Vines were planted across the empire to grow grapes to make into wine.

Timber
Forests were stripped of wood all over the empire.

Roman baths
Public bathing brought the Romans together.

Slaves
Many Romans owned slaves. Some slaves had to build Roman roads.

Amphitheatres
Open-air theatres entertained Romans across the empire.

Roman soldiers
The army kept the peace and defended the borders against enemy invasion.

Named after Emperor Hadrian, work on this wall began in **122** CE. It marked the north-west edge of the empire.

Hadrian's Wall

NORTH SEA

This leader of the Arverni tribe led an uprising against Roman power in **52** BCE.

The Romans built this lighthouse in modern-day Spain.

This was the most important gold mine in the Roman Empire.

Vercingetorix

Tower of Hercules

Las Medulas

Pont du Gard

The Appian Way le

Roman roads
The Romans built mar link the towns and citie paved roads helped so around the e

Verona Arena

The Romans built aqueducts to transport water from one place to another.

ATLANTIC OCEAN

Rome

Mount Vesuvius

MEDITERRANEAN SEA

The wa the vol Ves

Carthaginians

Theatre at Djemila

The Romans built th amphitheatre in modern-day Tunisia

The Carthaginians used war elephants to fight against the Roman Empire.

Julius Caesar
One of Ancient Rome's most well-known leaders, Julius Caesar, conquered large amounts of land for Rome. The empire began with his great-nephew, Augustus, who made himself the first emperor.

Leptis Magna

An importa in Roman L

SCALE

0 — 200 miles

0 — 200 kilometres

Picture symbols
You will find picture symbols without text plotted on some of the maps. Look at the key to find out what each symbol means.

Scale
The scale indicates the size of the country and the distances between different points on the map.

States at war

The five kingdoms each battled to become the most powerful. They were eventually united into the huge empire of China.

These mini maps show you where an area is in the world.

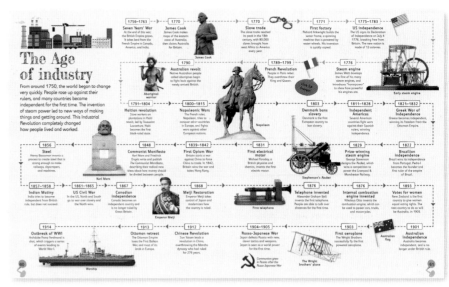

The Age of industry

From around 1750, the world began to change very quickly. People rose up against their rulers, and many countries became independent for the first time. The invention of steam power led to new ways of making things and getting around. This Industrial Revolution completely changed how people lived and worked.

Timelines

Each chapter starts with a timeline spread. The timelines show you events in different parts of the world, in the order they happened.

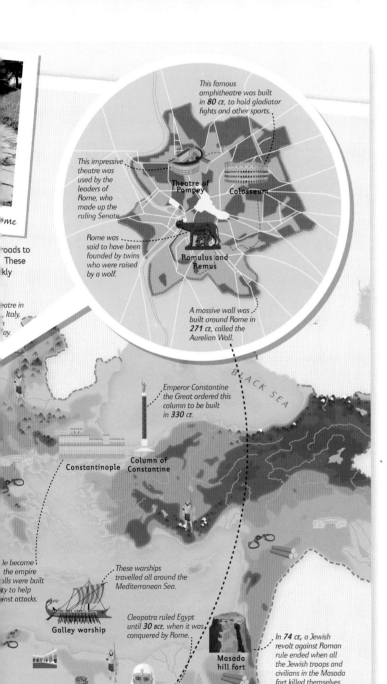

This famous amphitheatre was built in **80 CE**, to hold gladiator fights and other sports.

This impressive theatre was used by the leaders of Rome, who made up the ruling Senate.

Rome was said to have been founded by twins who were raised by a wolf.

A massive wall was built around Rome in **271 CE**, called the Aurelian Wall.

Emperor Constantine the Great ordered this column to be built in **330 CE**.

These warships travelled all around the Mediterranean Sea.

Cleopatra ruled Egypt until **30 BCE**, when it was conquered by Rome.

In **74 CE**, a Jewish revolt against Roman rule ended when all the Jewish troops and civilians in the Masada fort killed themselves.

Masada hill fort

Galley warship

Cleopatra

Constantinople

Column of Constantine

BLACK SEA

Theatre of Pompey

Colosseum

Romulus and Remus

How years are numbered

Each year is given a number, to help people keep track of what happened (and happens) when. These numbers are called dates. Here are some things that are useful to know about historical dates.

CE and BCE

You will see that some dates have "CE" or "BCE" after them. CE means "common era" and BCE means "before the common era". CE is used for dates after the year 1 BCE, and BCE for dates before 1 CE. In this book, where a date doesn't have CE or BCE after it, it is CE.

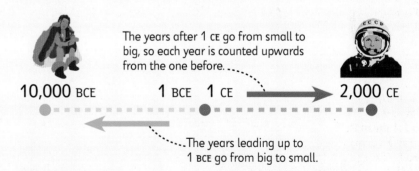

The years after 1 CE go from small to big, so each year is counted upwards from the one before.

10,000 BCE   1 BCE   1 CE   2,000 CE

The years leading up to 1 BCE go from big to small.

Centuries

A century is a period of 100 years. Historians often talk about periods of time using centuries, for example, "the 18th century". The years covered by a century are the 100 leading up to it. So the 18th century covers the years 1700–1799. Here are some examples.

Century	Time covered	Century	Time covered
14th century	1300–1399 CE	18th century	1700–1799 CE
15th century	1400–1499 CE	19th century	1800–1899 CE
16th century	1500–1599 CE	20th century	1900–1999 CE
17th century	1600–1699 CE	21st century	2000–2099 CE

Close-up map
These maps show extra detail of interesting areas that would be too small to show on the main maps.

Page numbers
The colour of the circle matches the chapter colour and tells you which chapter you are in.

World people

The human story began in Africa six million years ago, when apes began to walk upright on two legs. Over time, human-like apes, called hominins, grew bigger and more intelligent. Our species, *Homo sapiens*, appeared in Africa 200,000 years ago. Around 120,000 years ago, some of them left Africa to spread all over the world.

Firemaker

Homo erectus (upright man) was the first hominin to leave Africa, 1.8 million years ago. They were the same height as us, but their faces were more ape-like. They made stone axes and learned to control fire.

Homo erectus

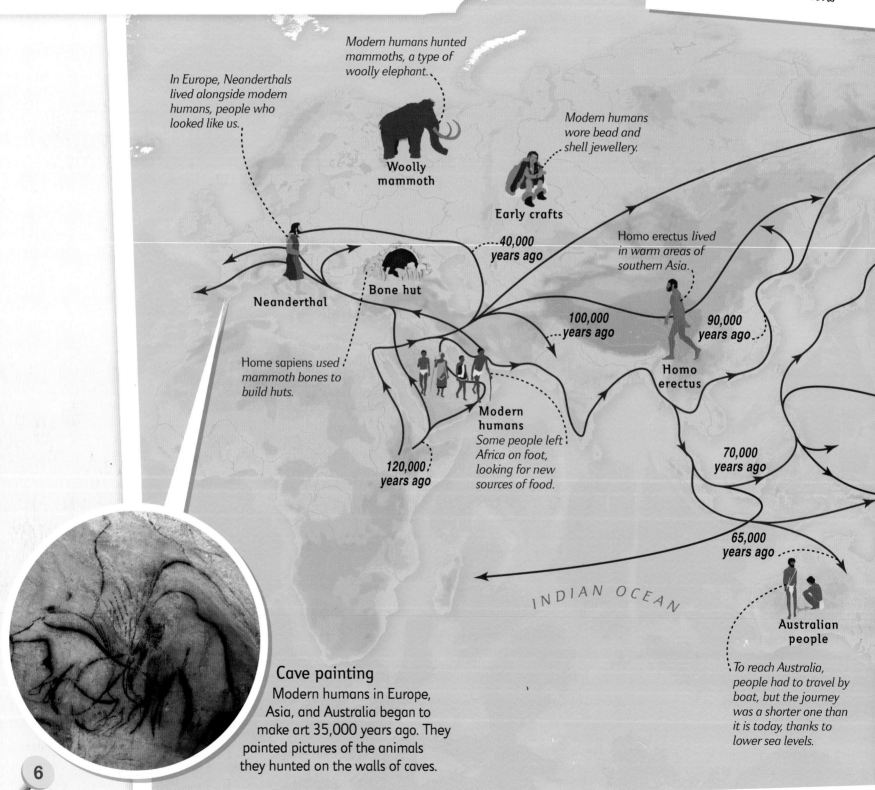

In Europe, Neanderthals lived alongside modern humans, people who looked like us.

Modern humans hunted mammoths, a type of woolly elephant.

Modern humans wore bead and shell jewellery.

Woolly mammoth

Early crafts

Homo erectus lived in warm areas of southern Asia.

Neanderthal

Bone hut

40,000 years ago

100,000 years ago

90,000 years ago

Home sapiens *used mammoth bones to build huts.*

Homo erectus

Modern humans
Some people left Africa on foot, looking for new sources of food.

120,000 years ago

70,000 years ago

65,000 years ago

INDIAN OCEAN

Australian people

To reach Australia, people had to travel by boat, but the journey was a shorter one than it is today, thanks to lower sea levels.

Cave painting

Modern humans in Europe, Asia, and Australia began to make art 35,000 years ago. They painted pictures of the animals they hunted on the walls of caves.

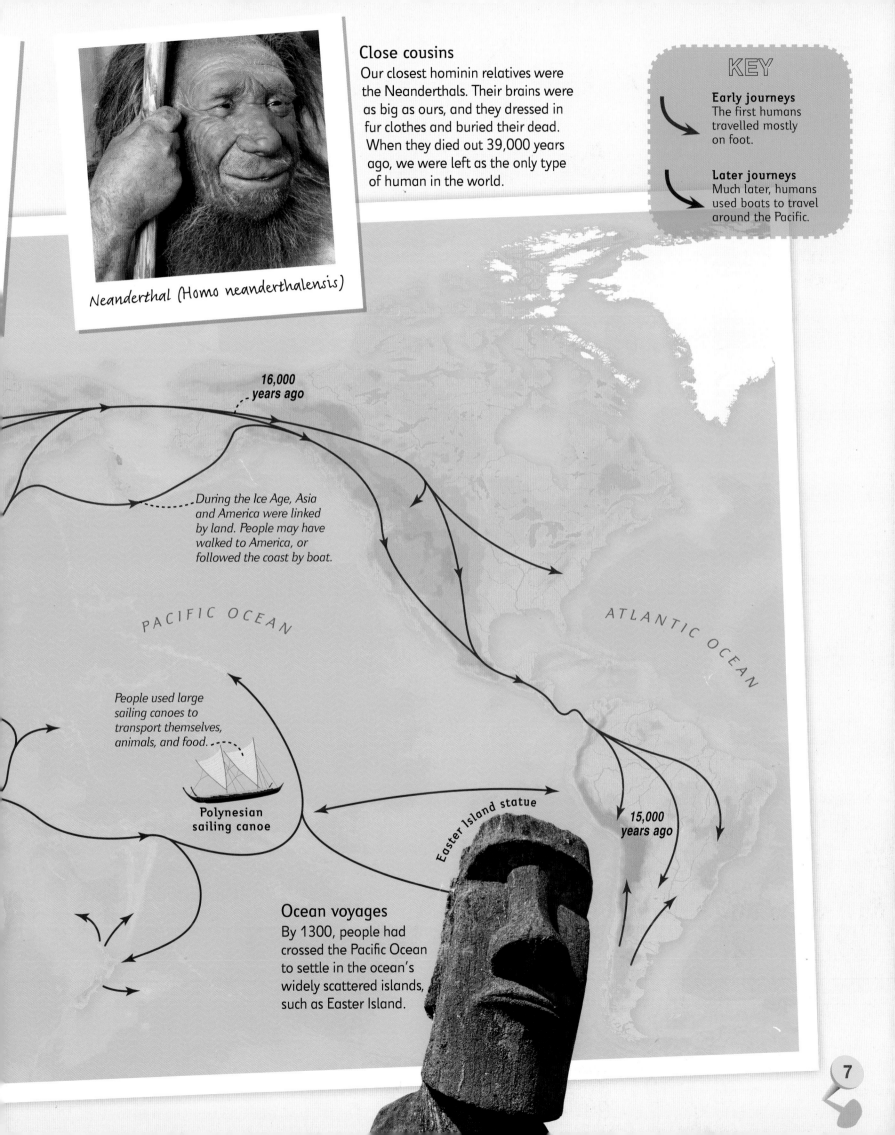

Close cousins
Our closest hominin relatives were the Neanderthals. Their brains were as big as ours, and they dressed in fur clothes and buried their dead. When they died out 39,000 years ago, we were left as the only type of human in the world.

Neanderthal (Homo neanderthalensis)

16,000 years ago

During the Ice Age, Asia and America were linked by land. People may have walked to America, or followed the coast by boat.

PACIFIC OCEAN

ATLANTIC OCEAN

People used large sailing canoes to transport themselves, animals, and food.

Polynesian sailing canoe

Easter Island statue

15,000 years ago

Ocean voyages
By 1300, people had crossed the Pacific Ocean to settle in the ocean's widely scattered islands, such as Easter Island.

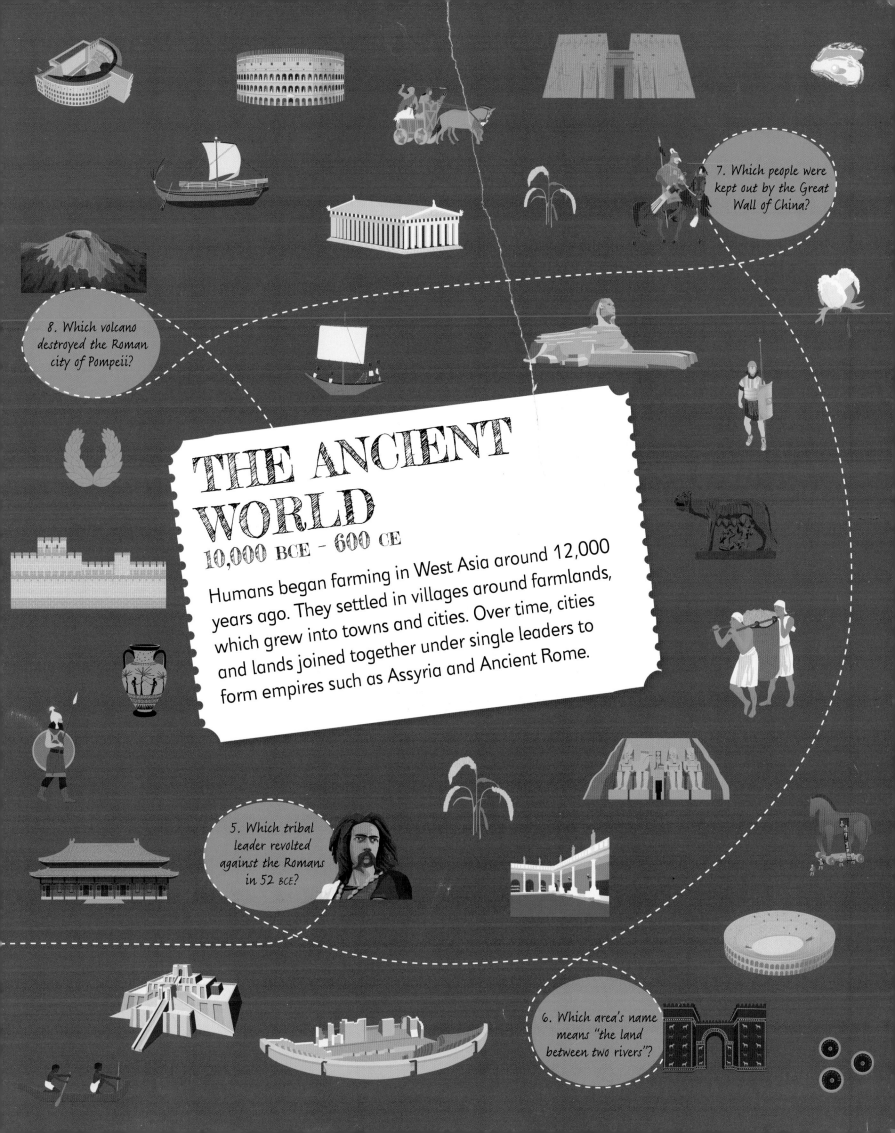

THE ANCIENT WORLD
10,000 BCE – 600 CE

Humans began farming in West Asia around 12,000 years ago. They settled in villages around farmlands, which grew into towns and cities. Over time, cities and lands joined together under single leaders to form empires such as Assyria and Ancient Rome.

7. Which people were kept out by the Great Wall of China?

8. Which volcano destroyed the Roman city of Pompeii?

5. Which tribal leader revolted against the Romans in 52 BCE?

6. Which area's name means "the land between two rivers"?

The Ancient World

For most of the past, people lived as hunter-gatherers. They moved around, hunted animals, and gathered wild plants. After the last Ice Age – a long period of cold weather – ended about 11,500 years ago, people learned how to farm. Planting crops and raising animals meant they had to settle down in one place. The number of people grew, and villages became towns. Soon states and empires were also created.

35,000 years ago

First art
People in Europe and Asia make the first works of art – cave paintings and carvings of animals and people.

5000 BCE

First metal tools
People in Europe and western Asia begin to make tools, such as axes, from copper rather than stone.

4000 BCE

World's first city
Villages at Uruk in Sumer (southern Iraq) join together to create the world's first city.

Bronze Age spear

2613–2503 BCE

Great Pyramids built
Egyptian pharaohs build huge pyramid tombs at Giza.

2500 BCE

Indus cities
The Indus, or Harappan, people build cities in the Indus valley of Northwest India. They also grow cotton for cloth.

2500 BCE

First recorded war
The first recorded war in history is fought, between the Sumerian cities of Lagash and Umma.

c.2300 BCE

First empire
King Sargon of Akkad conquers Mesopotamia and creates the world's first empire.

Pyramids at Giza

117 CE

Roman Empire
The Roman Empire reaches its largest size, under Emperor Trajan. It stretches from Spain in the west to Iraq in the east.

221–210 CE

China's first emperor
China is united under the First Emperor. When he dies, he is buried in a tomb protected by a terracotta (clay) army.

Terracotta army

14,000–9,000 years ago
The climate warms
The world gets warmer, sea levels rise, and forests spread. Big animals, such as mammoths, die out.

Woolly mammoth

13,000 BCE
Pottery invented
The Jomon people of Japan make the world's oldest known pottery.

Jomon pot

6500 BCE
Earliest silk-making
Silk begins to be spun in China. Silk is a fine fabric made from the cocoons of the silk moth.

Silk worms

7000 BCE
First cloth woven
People in the Fertile Crescent learn to weave cloth from the fibres of a plant called flax.

10,000 BCE
Farming begins
In the Fertile Crescent, stretching from Egypt to Iraq, people begin to plant wheat and barley, and raise animals for meat and milk.

3300 BCE
Writing invented
Egyptians invent the world's first writing system, hieroglyphs.

Egyptian hieroglyphs

3100 BCE
Egypt united
Egypt becomes a single kingdom, under the rule of a pharaoh, perhaps called Narmer.

3000 BCE
Bronze Age begins
Mesopotamians mix tin and copper to make bronze, a harder metal. Soon after, bronze is also made in China.

3000 BCE
South American farming begins
Farming starts in the Andes mountains of South America, where people grow crops including potatoes.

South American potatoes

King Sargon

c.1200 BCE
Iron Age begins
The Bronze Age ends and the Iron Age begins when people in Anatolia (modern Turkey) start making iron.

c.1200 BCE
First American civilizations
The Olmecs of Mesoamerica and the people of Chavin de Huantar in Peru live in the first American civilizations.

c.1000–500 BCE
Farming spreads in Africa
Farming people move from Nigeria to settle across much of Africa. They grow yams, millet, and sorghum. From 400 BCE, they make iron tools.

334–323 BCE
Alexander the Great
After uniting Greece, Alexander the Great of Macedon conquers an empire stretching from Egypt to India.

c.500–336 BCE
Ancient Greece
Greek civilization is at its peak. The Greeks create beautiful art and architecture, and invent science, philosophy, theatre, history writing, and politics.

Stonehenge

Farming people worked together to set up huge monuments called megaliths, meaning "great stones". Some were tombs to bury the dead. Others, such as Stonehenge in Britain, were places for religious ceremonies.

Settling down

Farming began in Asia and then moved into Europe. People settled down in different places and started a variety of cultures.

Orkney

Funnelbeaker

Newgrange

In 10,000 BCE, Britain was joined onto Europe. Later, around 6500 BCE, rising sea levels flooded this area, cutting Britain off.

In Denmark and Sweden, people made pots with funnel-shaped tops, called funnelbeakers.

In Central Europe, people decorated pots by scratching lines on the clay.

Early trade

After people settled down as farmers, they began to make things to trade, such as pots. The most prized objects for trading were polished stone axes, made from around 4000 BCE. They were traded across long distances.

Salisbury

Carnac

Carnac stones

In Southern Europe, people decorated pots with cockle shells. Cardium is the Latin name for a cockle.

Linear pottery

Cardium pottery

Polished flint axes

TYRRHENIAN SEA

The Stone Age

The earliest period of our history is called the Stone Age, because people used tools made from stone. They hunted wild animals and gathered wild plants. Later, from around 10,000 BCE, people in East Asia began to plant crops and keep animals. Farming then spread west across Europe.

SCALE

0   200 miles

0   200 kilometres

Malta

NORTH SEA

ATLANTIC SEA

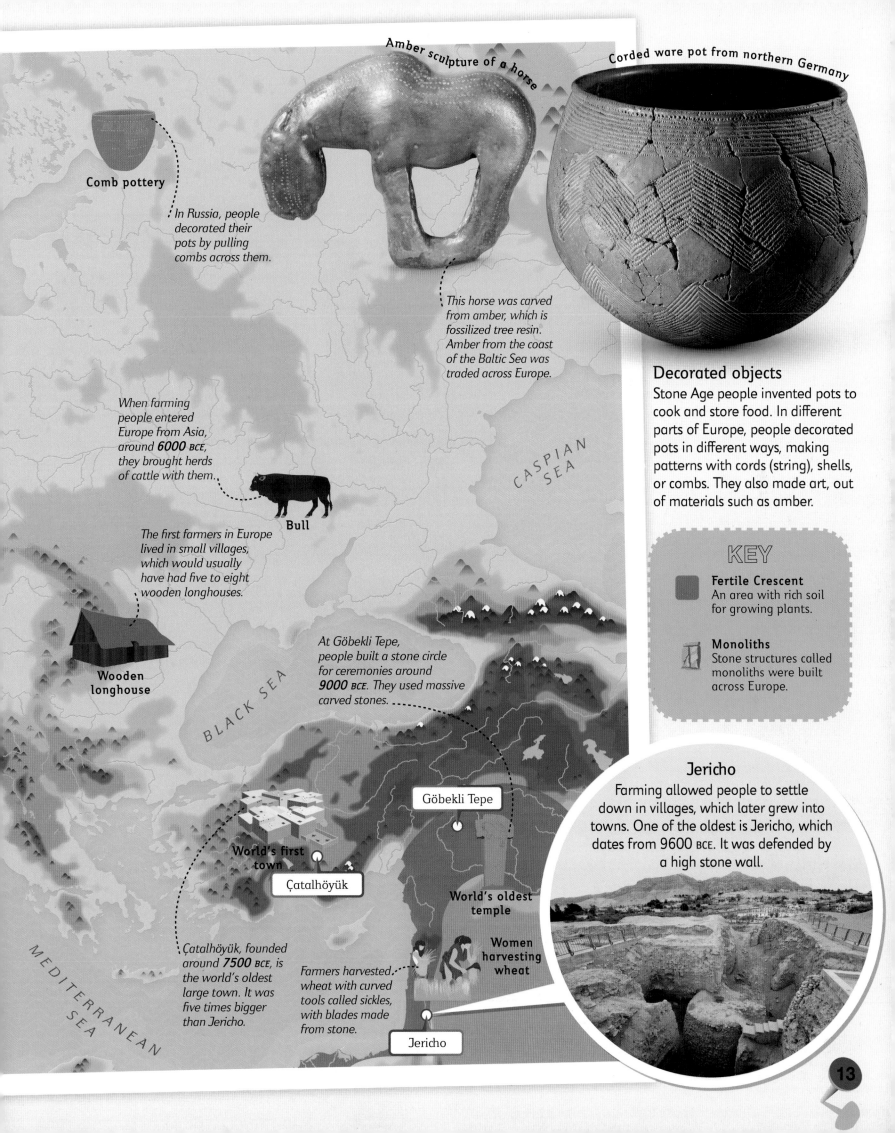

Comb pottery

In Russia, people decorated their pots by pulling combs across them.

Amber sculpture of a horse

This horse was carved from amber, which is fossilized tree resin. Amber from the coast of the Baltic Sea was traded across Europe.

Corded ware pot from northern Germany

Decorated objects

Stone Age people invented pots to cook and store food. In different parts of Europe, people decorated pots in different ways, making patterns with cords (string), shells, or combs. They also made art, out of materials such as amber.

*When farming people entered Europe from Asia, around **6000** BCE, they brought herds of cattle with them.*

Bull

CASPIAN SEA

The first farmers in Europe lived in small villages, which would usually have had five to eight wooden longhouses.

Wooden longhouse

BLACK SEA

*At Göbekli Tepe, people built a stone circle for ceremonies around **9000** BCE. They used massive carved stones.*

KEY

■ **Fertile Crescent**
An area with rich soil for growing plants.

⌐ **Monoliths**
Stone structures called monoliths were built across Europe.

Göbekli Tepe

World's first town

Çatalhöyük

World's oldest temple

Women harvesting wheat

*Çatalhöyük, founded around **7500** BCE, is the world's oldest large town. It was five times bigger than Jericho.*

Farmers harvested wheat with curved tools called sickles, with blades made from stone.

Jericho

MEDITERRANEAN SEA

Jericho

Farming allowed people to settle down in villages, which later grew into towns. One of the oldest is Jericho, which dates from 9600 BCE. It was defended by a high stone wall.

Mesopotamia

Mesopotamia means "the land between the two rivers". It existed around the rivers Tigris and Euphrates in the Middle East. It was here, around 3300 BCE, that the world's first cities were built. Mesopotamian cities were ruled by kings, who waged war with each other using trained armies. The Mesopotamians invented bronze-making and writing.

Writing

Mesopotamians invented one of the first writing systems. It is called cuneiform, which means "wedge-shaped". It was written by pushing a sharp reed into a soft clay tablet. Cuneiform was used for 3,200 years across western Asia.

Cuneiform writing

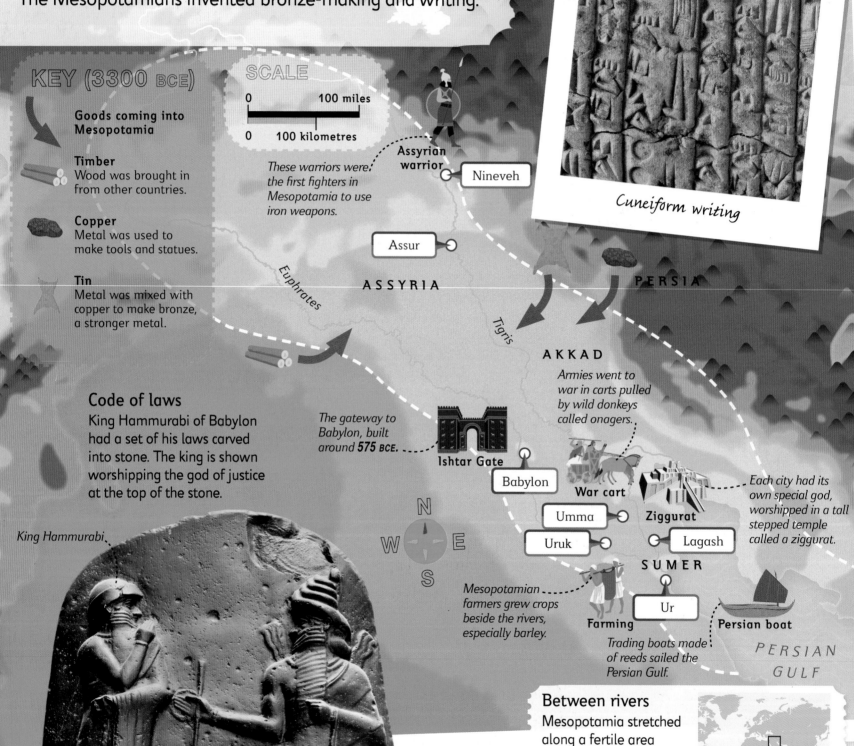

KEY (3300 BCE)

Goods coming into Mesopotamia

Timber
Wood was brought in from other countries.

Copper
Metal was used to make tools and statues.

Tin
Metal was mixed with copper to make bronze, a stronger metal.

SCALE

0 — 100 miles

0 — 100 kilometres

These warriors were the first fighters in Mesopotamia to use iron weapons.

Assyrian warrior

Nineveh

Assur

ASSYRIA

PERSIA

Euphrates

Tigris

AKKAD

Armies went to war in carts pulled by wild donkeys called onagers.

Code of laws

King Hammurabi of Babylon had a set of his laws carved into stone. The king is shown worshipping the god of justice at the top of the stone.

King Hammurabi

The gateway to Babylon, built around 575 BCE.

Ishtar Gate

Babylon

War cart

Ziggurat

Each city had its own special god, worshipped in a tall stepped temple called a ziggurat.

Umma

Uruk

Lagash

SUMER

Mesopotamian farmers grew crops beside the rivers, especially barley.

Farming

Ur

Persian boat

Trading boats made of reeds sailed the Persian Gulf.

PERSIAN GULF

Shamash, god of justice

Between rivers

Mesopotamia stretched along a fertile area between the Tigris and Euphrates, which made it a good place to farm.

Indus Valley

The land around the Indus River was the birthplace of another of the first civilizations. From about 2600 BCE, people here built carefully planned cities. This was the largest early civilization, bigger than Egypt and Mesopotamia put together. There is no evidence left of how the people of the Indus Valley were ruled.

Indus seal

The people of the Indus Valley invented a type of writing with around 300 picture signs, which we still cannot understand. It was used on carved stone seals, where the signs appeared above pictures of animals.

Ruins of Mohenjo-Daro

The biggest Indus city was Mohenjo-Daro. Every house had its own water supply, toilet, and bath.

KEY (2600 BCE)

Goods coming into the Indus area

Silver
This metal was used to make jewellery.

Copper
This metal used to make pots and knives.

Lapis lazuli
This blue stone from Afghanistan was used to make jewellery.

Tin
This metal was mixed with copper to make bronze.

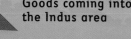

Cotton growing
Cotton fibres were woven into cloth.

Harappa

Indus

Indus boat

Mohenjo-Daro

Carnelian

A red stone called carnelian was used to make beads for jewellery.

Indus traders travelled by boat, taking goods along the rivers.

THAR DESERT

Elephants were hunted for their ivory tusks.

Asian elephant

Dholavira

N
W E
S

Coastal people collected oysters to get the pearls sometimes found inside.

Pearls

Lothal

A R A B I A N
S E A

SCALE

0   100 miles

0   100 kilometres

River network

The Indus civilization grew up around small rivers that flowed into the large Indus River, which ended at the Arabian Sea.

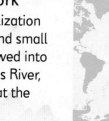

15

Ancient Egypt

Around 3000 BCE, the people who lived along the River Nile created one of the world's earliest civilizations, Ancient Egypt. Kings known as pharaohs ruled Egypt for over 3,000 years. It was the most stable and longest-lasting civilization in the ancient world.

Hieroglyphs

The Egyptians invented hieroglyphs, the world's first writing system. Hieroglyphs were pictures that stood for things and ideas. They were carved into stone or written on a type of paper called papyrus.

Hieroglyphs carved into stone

Fertile Nile

Egypt lies along the River Nile, which flows through the desert of north-east Africa into the Mediterranean Sea.

KEY (3000 – 1000 BCE)

Egyptian border
The dotted line shows the edge of Egypt.

Wheat
This was the main crop grown along the Nile.

Mud houses
People lived in houses made of mudbricks.

SCALE

```
0        250 miles
0        250 kilometres
```

MEDITERRANEAN SEA

LOWER EGYPT

Memphis

Sphinx at Giza

Giza

The Sphinx, a statue of a lion with a human head, guards the pyramids.

Farmers grew wheat and other crops next to the river.

Ploughing

Egyptian boats sailed south using the wind, which usually blows from north to south. The current carried them north again.

Sailing south

Pyramids of Giza

From 2650 to 1800 BCE, pharaohs were buried in huge stone tombs called pyramids. The Great Pyramid is the only survivor of the seven wonders of the world.

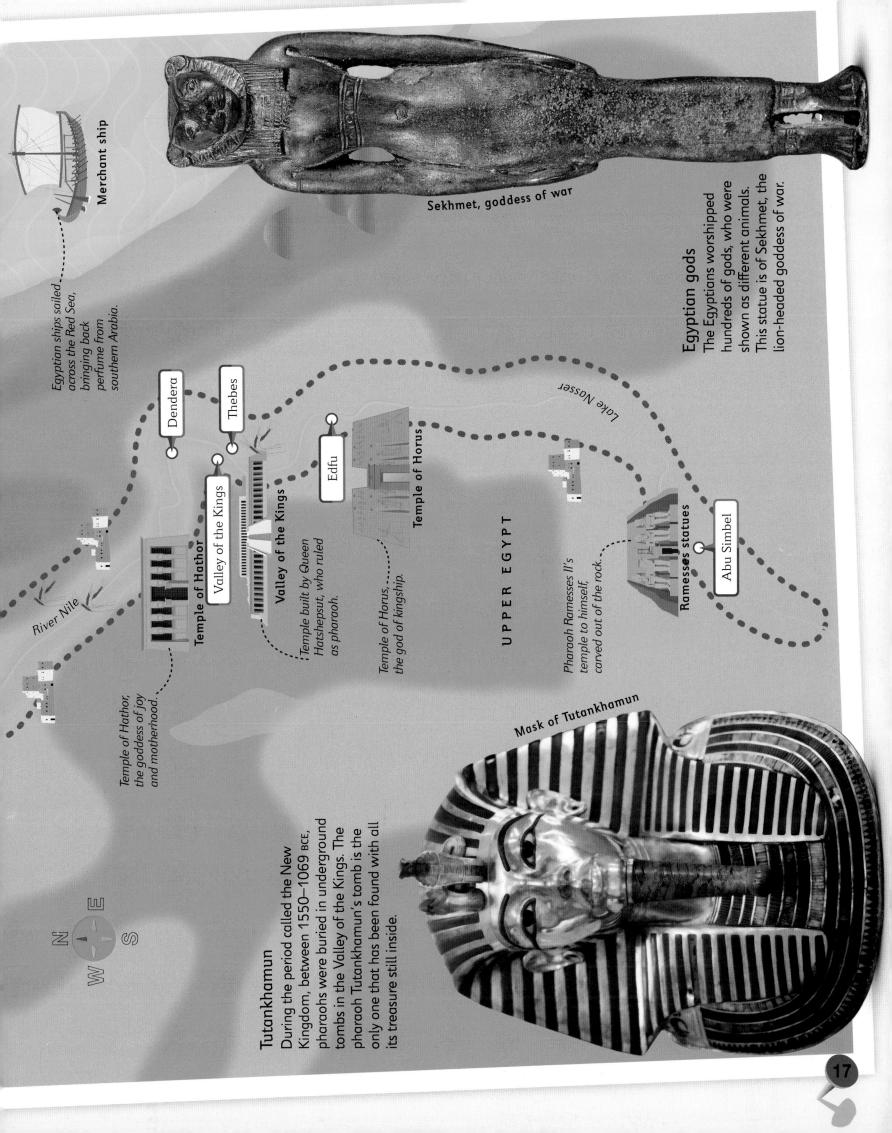

Merchant ship

Sekhmet, goddess of war

Egyptian ships sailed across the Red Sea, bringing back perfume from southern Arabia.

Egyptian gods
The Egyptians worshipped hundreds of gods, who were shown as different animals. This statue is of Sekhmet, the lion-headed goddess of war.

Dendera

Thebes

Lake Nasser

Valley of the Kings

Edfu

Temple of Horus

Temple of Hathor

Temple of Hathor, the goddess of joy and motherhood.

Temple built by Queen Hatshepsut, who ruled as pharaoh.

Temple of Horus, the god of kingship.

River Nile

UPPER EGYPT

Ramesses statues

Pharaoh Ramesses II's temple to himself, carved out of the rock.

Abu Simbel

Tutankhamun
During the period called the New Kingdom, between 1550–1069 BCE, pharaohs were buried in underground tombs in the Valley of the Kings. The pharaoh Tutankhamun's tomb is the only one that has been found with all its treasure still inside.

Mask of Tutankhamun

N
W E
S

KEY

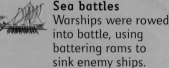
City-states
ATHENS
Individual Greek cities ruled themselves and had their own armies.

Merchant routes
Greek merchants sailed the seas, carrying goods such as olive oil.

Sea battles
Warships were rowed into battle, using battering rams to sink enemy ships.

Greek games
Athletic contests were held in religious centres, such as Olympia.

Many cities
Ancient Greece was a collection of city-states. The Greeks travelled and founded cities all over the Mediterranean.

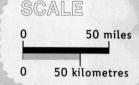
SCALE
0   50 miles
0   50 kilometres

NAPLES

PAESTUM

Far and wide
The Greeks founded settlements all around the Mediterranean and the Black Sea. The best surviving Greek temples are not in Greece but in Italy. This one is in Sicily.

N
W   E
S

IONIAN SEA

Temple of Segesta, built c.420 BCE

The Olympic Games
The Greeks invented athletic competitions. The most famous was held at Olympia, during a festival in honour of Zeus, king of the gods. Athletes came from all over the Greek world.

SYRACUSE

Ancient Greece

The Ancient Greeks were some of the most creative people in history. They invented theatre, sport, politics, science, and the writing of history. Their beautiful art and architecture is still copied today. Ancient Greek civilization was at its height between 500 and 300 BCE.

Wrestling in the Greek Olympics

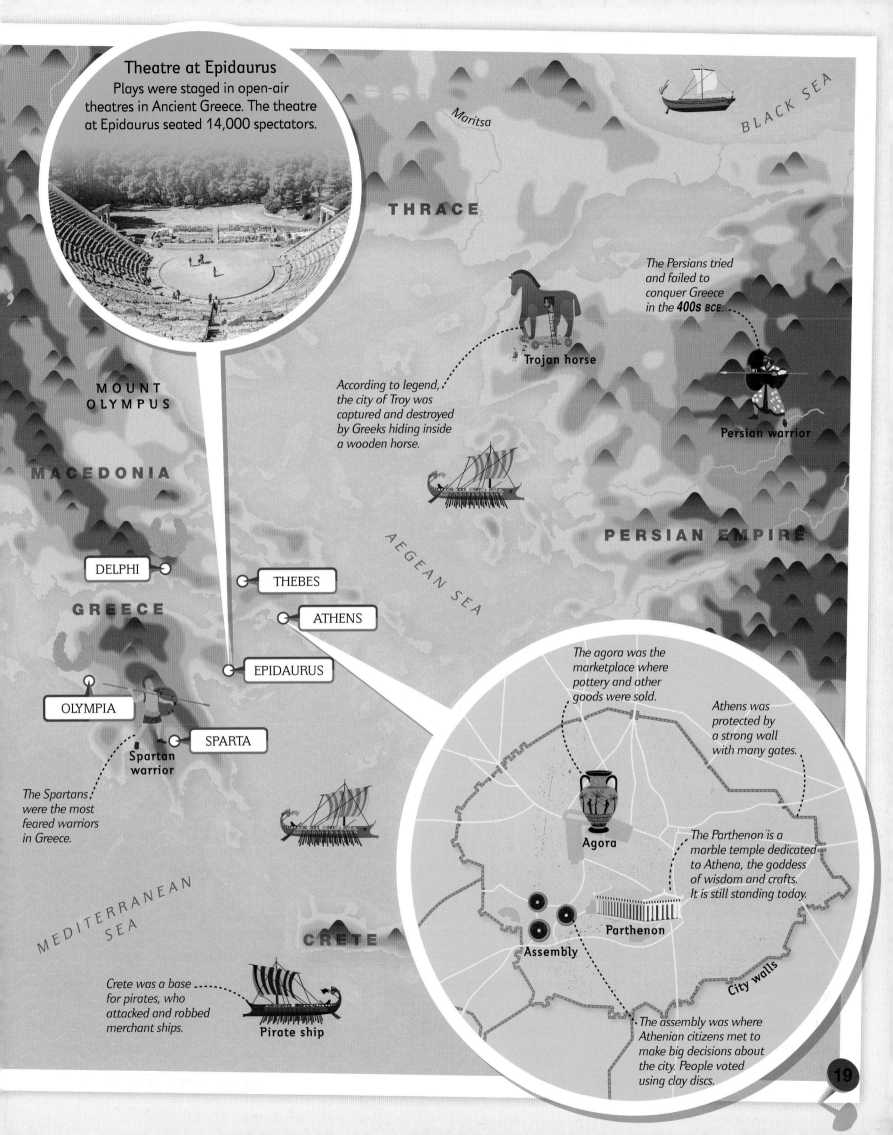

Theatre at Epidaurus
Plays were staged in open-air theatres in Ancient Greece. The theatre at Epidaurus seated 14,000 spectators.

Maritsa

BLACK SEA

THRACE

MOUNT OLYMPUS

MACEDONIA

*The Persians tried and failed to conquer Greece in the **400s** BCE.*

Trojan horse

According to legend, the city of Troy was captured and destroyed by Greeks hiding inside a wooden horse.

Persian warrior

PERSIAN EMPIRE

AEGEAN SEA

DELPHI

GREECE

THEBES

ATHENS

EPIDAURUS

OLYMPIA

SPARTA

Spartan warrior

The Spartans were the most feared warriors in Greece.

MEDITERRANEAN SEA

CRETE

Crete was a base for pirates, who attacked and robbed merchant ships.

Pirate ship

The agora was the marketplace where pottery and other goods were sold.

Athens was protected by a strong wall with many gates.

Agora

The Parthenon is a marble temple dedicated to Athena, the goddess of wisdom and crafts. It is still standing today.

Parthenon

Assembly

City walls

The assembly was where Athenian citizens met to make big decisions about the city. People voted using clay discs.

Ancient China

From 475 BCE, China was divided into several kingdoms, which were always at war with each other. This time, called the Warring States period, ended in 221 BCE, when the king of Qin conquered all his rivals. He ruled as China's First Emperor. Qin, pronounced "Chin", gave its name to all of China.

Kingdoms at war
The many warring states each battled to become the most powerful. They were eventually united into the huge empire of China.

First Emperor of China
Ying Zheng, known as the First Emperor, ruled China harshly from 221–210 BCE. He forced everybody in the country to work for him. People had to build roads, canals, a great wall, and a huge tomb for him.

The First Emperor

Terracotta Army
In 210 BCE, the First Emperor was buried in a human-made mountain. Nearby, an army of more than 7,000 life-size terracotta (pottery) warriors was also buried.

Terracotta soldiers

The First Emperor built a road 800 km (500 miles) long, from Xianyang to Mongolia.

N
W E
S

The Straight Road

Xianyang

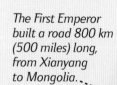

Epang palace

The capital of China was the city of Xianyang. The First Emperor built a palace here.

QIN

Chariot

Government officials travelled around in horse-drawn chariots.

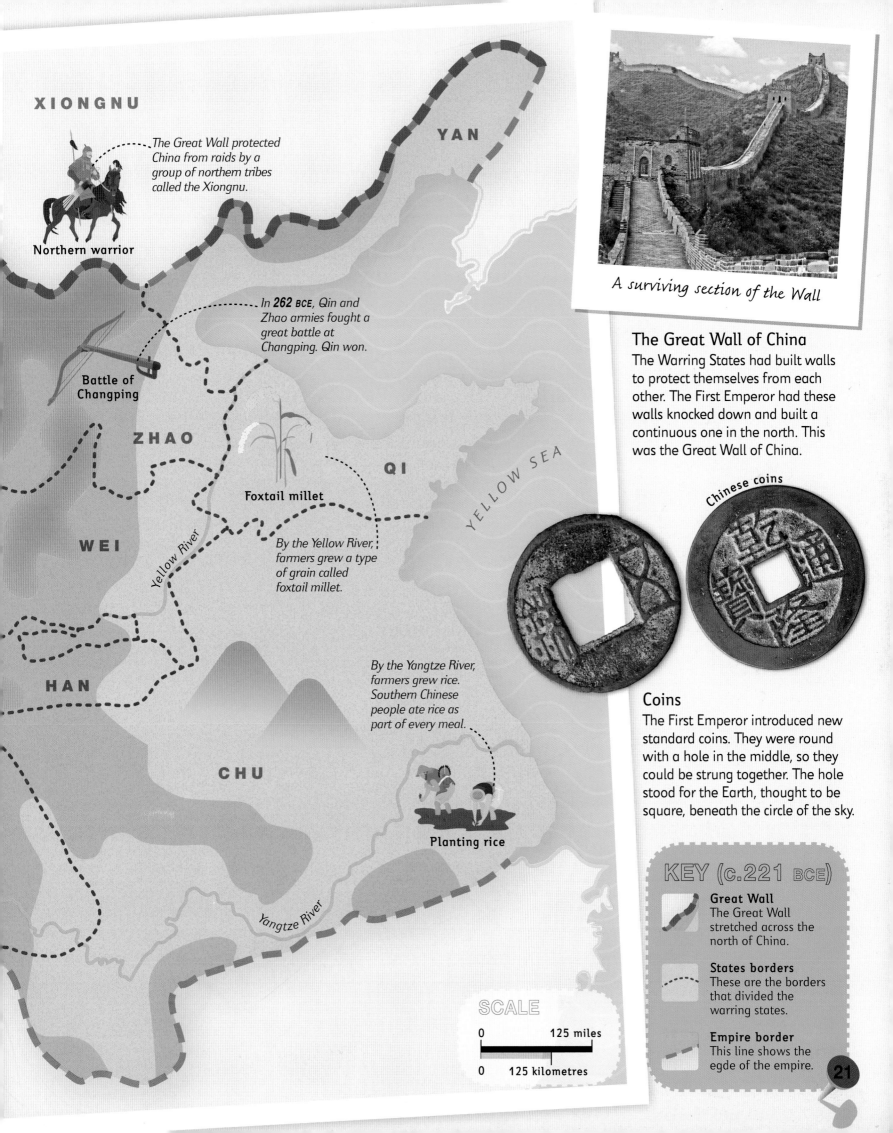

XIONGNU

The Great Wall protected China from raids by a group of northern tribes called the Xiongnu.

Northern warrior

YAN

A surviving section of the Wall

In **262** BCE, Qin and Zhao armies fought a great battle at Changping. Qin won.

Battle of Changping

ZHAO

Foxtail millet

QI

By the Yellow River, farmers grew a type of grain called foxtail millet.

YELLOW SEA

Yellow River

WEI

HAN

By the Yangtze River, farmers grew rice. Southern Chinese people ate rice as part of every meal.

CHU

Planting rice

Yangtze River

The Great Wall of China

The Warring States had built walls to protect themselves from each other. The First Emperor had these walls knocked down and built a continuous one in the north. This was the Great Wall of China.

Chinese coins

Coins

The First Emperor introduced new standard coins. They were round with a hole in the middle, so they could be strung together. The hole stood for the Earth, thought to be square, beneath the circle of the sky.

SCALE

0   125 miles

0   125 kilometres

KEY (c.221 BCE)

Great Wall
The Great Wall stretched across the north of China.

States borders
These are the borders that divided the warring states.

Empire border
This line shows the egde of the empire.

21

Ancient Rome

More than 2,000 years ago, Ancient Rome was one of the most powerful nations in the world. At first, Rome was ruled by kings. It became a republic in 509 BCE, which meant that it was ruled by members of Roman society. In 27 BCE Rome became an empire, led by a ruler called an emperor. At its largest, in 117 CE, the Roman Empire was home to more than 65 million people.

Punic Wars

Between 264 and 146 BCE, Rome fought three wars against the city of Carthage in modern-day Tunisia. They wanted control of the Mediterranean Sea. The wars, known as the Punic Wars, ended in total Roman victory.

General Hannibal from Carthage

KEY (c.117 CE)

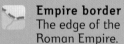

Empire border
The edge of the Roman Empire.

Grain
Shipped to Rome from North Africa and Sicily.

Grapevines
Vines were planted across the empire to grow grapes to make into wine.

Timber
Forests were stripped of wood all over the empire.

Roman baths
Public bathing brought the Romans together.

Slaves
Many Romans owned slaves. Some slaves had to build Roman roads.

Amphitheatres
Open-air theatres entertained Romans across the empire.

Roman soldiers
The army kept the peace and defended the borders against enemy invasion.

Named after Emperor Hadrian, work on this wall began in *122* CE. It marked the north-west edge of the empire.

Hadrian's Wall

NORTH SEA

This leader of the Arverni tribe led an uprising against Roman power in *52* BCE.

The Romans built this lighthouse in modern-day Spain.

Vercingetorix

This was the most important gold mine in the Roman Empire.

Tower of Hercules

Las Medulas

Pont du Gard

The Romans built aqueducts to transport water from one place to another.

ATLANTIC OCEAN

MEDITERRANEAN SEA

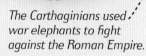

Carthaginians

The Carthaginians used war elephants to fight against the Roman Empire.

Julius Caesar

One of Ancient Rome's most well-known leaders, Julius Caesar, conquered large amounts of land for Rome. The empire began with his great-nephew, Augustus, who made himself the first emperor.

The Appian Way leading out of Rome

Roman roads

The Romans built many long, straight roads to link the towns and cities of the empire. These paved roads helped soldiers move quickly around the empire.

This famous amphitheatre was built in *80 CE*, to hold gladiator fights and other sports.

This impressive theatre was used by the leaders of Rome, who made up the ruling Senate.

Theatre of Pompey

Colosseum

Rome was said to have been founded by twins who were raised by a wolf.

Romulus and Remus

A massive wall was built around Rome in *271 CE*, called the Aurelian Wall.

This theatre in Verona, Italy, is still in use today.

Verona Arena

BLACK SEA

Emperor Constantine the Great ordered this column to be built in *330 CE*.

Rome

Mount Vesuvius

Constantinople

Column of Constantine

The city of Pompeii was destroyed by the eruption of the volcano Mount Vesuvius in *79 CE*.

Theatre at Djemila

The Romans built this amphitheatre in modern-day Tunisia.

Constantinople became the capital of the empire in *330 CE*. Walls were built around the city to help defend it against attacks.

These warships travelled all around the Mediterranean Sea.

An important city in Roman Libya.

Galley warship

Cleopatra ruled Egypt until *30 BCE*, when it was conquered by Rome.

In *74 CE*, a Jewish revolt against Roman rule ended when all the Jewish troops and civilians in the Masada fort killed themselves.

Leptis Magna

Masada hill fort

SCALE

0   200 miles

0   200 kilometres

Cleopatra

23

Judaism

The faith of the Jewish people, called Judaism, was the first religion that worshipped one God. Jews believe that God chose them as a special holy people, and gave them a set of laws to follow.

Torah reading in a synagogue

Islam

Muslims worship a single God, called Allah. Every year, millions of Muslims travel to their holy city of Mecca in a special journey called the Hajj.

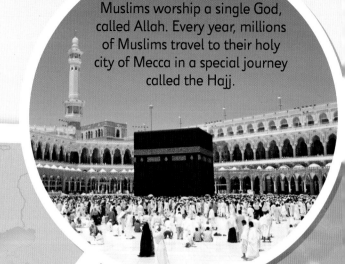

The Cross

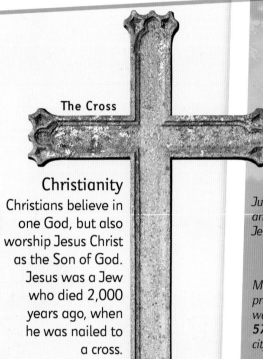

Christianity

Christians believe in one God, but also worship Jesus Christ as the Son of God. Jesus was a Jew who died 2,000 years ago, when he was nailed to a cross.

Christianity began in Jerusalem, where Jesus died.

Christianity

Jerusalem

Judaism

Judaism began in ancient Israel, the Jewish homeland.

Mecca

Mecca, where the prophet Muhammad was born around 570 CE, is the holiest city in Islam.

Islam

Sikhism comes from northern India, where Guru Nanak was born.

Sikhism

Nankana Sahib

Lumbini

Hinduism

Hinduism began in ancient India. Its sacred texts, the Vedas, were written down around 1200 BCE.

Buddhism

Buddhism began in northeast India, where the Buddha was born in 563 BCE.

INDIAN OCEAN

African religious mask

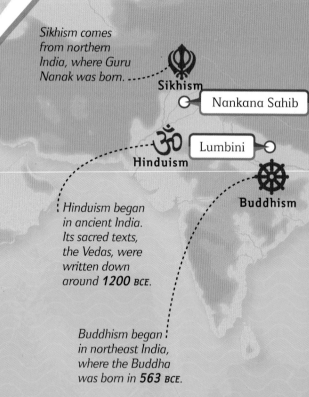

World religions

A religion is a set of beliefs about how to live a good life and what happens after death. In the past, there have been hundreds of different religions. Then, people began to follow larger, organised religions. Today, most people belong to only a few world religions.

Smaller religions

Alongside the major religions, there are still many smaller ones. In some parts of Africa, people believe in powerful spirits. They try to get the help of the spirits by dancing while wearing masks.

Sikhism

Sikhism was founded 500 years ago by an Indian teacher called Guru Nanak. He taught that there is one God, who can be worshipped anywhere, and that all humans are equal.

Guru Nanak, founder of Sikhism

Statue of the Hindu god Ganesh

Hinduism

Hinduism, the ancient religion of India, is practised in many different ways. Hindus worship hundreds of gods. One of the most popular is Ganesh, who has an elephant's head.

ASIA

Shinto
Buddhism

Shinto is an ancient Japanese religion. Its followers worship gods and spirits of the natural world.

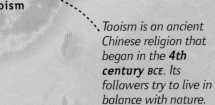

Taoism

Taoism is an ancient Chinese religion that began in the 4th century BCE. Its followers try to live in balance with nature.

PACIFIC OCEAN

KEY

Islam
A crescent moon and star.

Buddhism
A wheel with eight spokes.

Taoism
This symbol shows two opposites in balance.

Christianity
The cross on which Jesus died.

Shinto
A torii, or sacred gateway.

Judaism
The star of David, who was a Jewish king.

Sikhism
A khanda (set of swords).

Hinduism
A symbol for "om", a sacred sound.

World of faiths

The world's major religions all began in Asia and the Middle East, then spread to the rest of the world.

Buddhism

Buddhism was founded in northeast India 2,500 years ago, by a teacher called the Buddha (left). Unlike other religions, it is not based on a belief in gods. The goal of Buddhism is to find true wisdom.

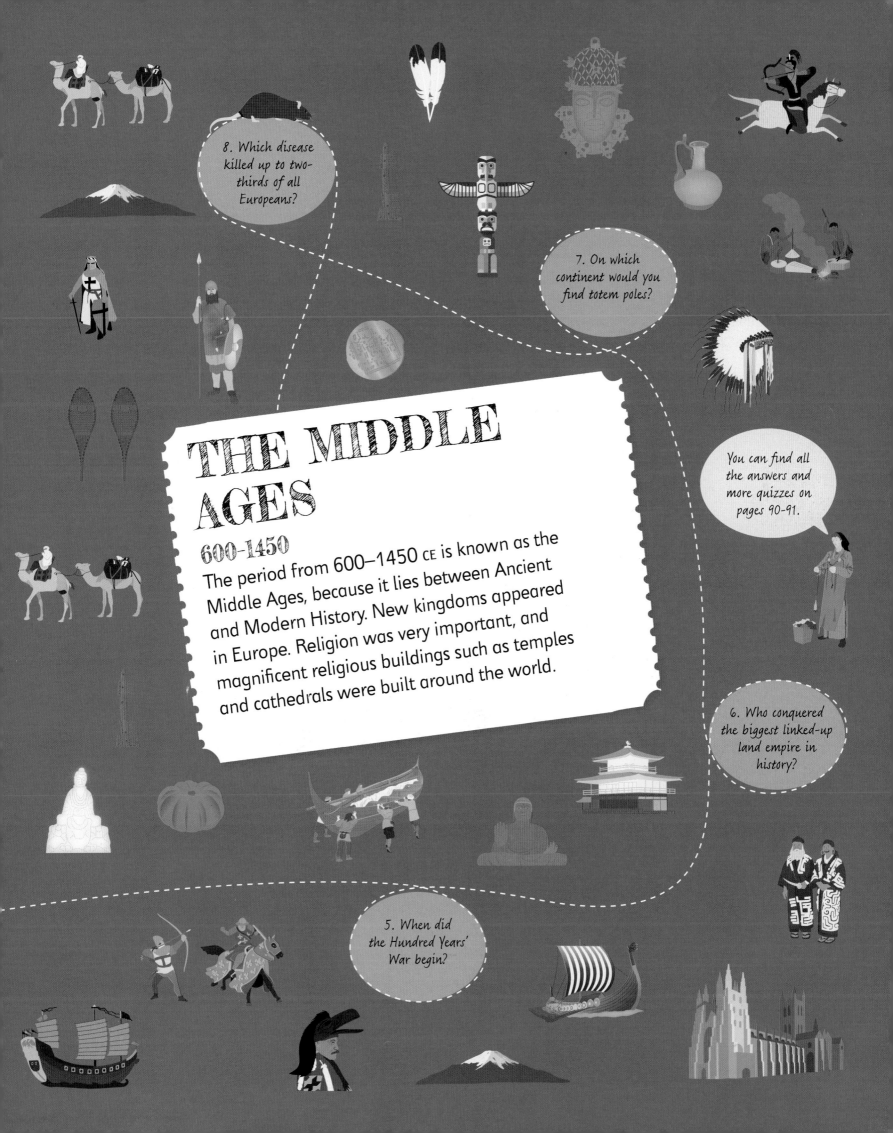

8. Which disease killed up to two-thirds of all Europeans?

7. On which continent would you find totem poles?

You can find all the answers and more quizzes on pages 90–91.

THE MIDDLE AGES

600–1450

The period from 600–1450 CE is known as the Middle Ages, because it lies between Ancient and Modern History. New kingdoms appeared in Europe. Religion was very important, and magnificent religious buildings such as temples and cathedrals were built around the world.

6. Who conquered the biggest linked-up land empire in history?

5. When did the Hundred Years' War begin?

Middle Ages

The Middle Ages saw the rise of many new kingdoms and empires. After the fall of the Roman Empire, several kingdoms appeared in Europe, sharing a strong belief in Christianity. The Middle Ages also saw the rise of a new world religion, Islam.

250–950
Maya civilization
The Mayan civilization, a collection of competing cities in Mesoamerica, is at its height.

Mayan writing carved on bone

711–721
Muslim Spain
A North African Muslim army invades and conquers Spain. The Muslims then move into France, but are defeated at the Battle of Poitiers in 732.

700
First American towns
The first towns are built in North America, in the eastern woodlands, by people known as the Mound Builders.

762
Baghdad
Caliph al-Mansur founds Baghdad as a new capital of the Islamic Empire, beginning the "Golden Age" of Islam.

William the Conqueror leading his men

1066
Norman conquest
The Normans, under William the Conqueror, conquer England. To control their English subjects, they later build many castles.

1095–1099
First Crusade
The First Crusade is a holy war fought by European armies against the Muslims who rule the Holy Land. The crusaders capture Jerusalem, and start Christian kingdoms.

1200–1350
Mali Empire
Growth of the Mali Empire, which conquers Ghana. The capital, Timbuktu, is famed for its wealth and the learning of its Islamic scholars.

1206–1294
Mongol conquests
The Mongols of East Asia conquer an empire stretching from eastern Europe to the Pacific Ocean. It is the biggest joined-up land empire in history.

1440–1473
Benin Empire founded
Reign of Oba (king) Ewuare the Great, founder of the Benin Empire of West Africa.

Queen mother of Benin

1420–1446
Dome of Florence
The Italian architect Filippo Brunelleschi builds the dome of the cathedral in Florence.

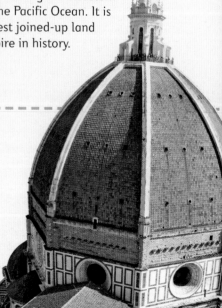

Dome of Florence Cathedral

c.500–600
First West African State
Rise of the Kingdom of Ghana, the first known state in West Africa. Its wealth comes from gold, traded across the Sahara with North Africa.

622–632
Birth of Islam
In Arabia, Muhammad, the founder of Islam, unites the previously divided Arab tribes under his rule.

618–907
Tang Dynasty
Under the Tang dynasty, the Chinese conquer a great empire, including much of Central Asia. Chang'an, the capital, is the world's biggest city.

Flag of Korea

668
Korea unified
King Munmu of Silla unites Korea, which was previously divided into separate kingdoms.

632–690
Arab conquests
The Arabs conquer the Persian Empire and North Africa.

Tang Dynasty, model of a polo player

789
First Viking raid
The Vikings stage their first attack on Britain, beginning more than a century of raiding.

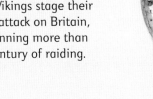

Viking axe and shield

800
Carolingian Empire
Pope Leo III crowns the Frankish (French) king, Charlemagne, as emperor. Charlemagne unites much of western Europe in his Carolingian Empire.

Statue of Leif Erikson in Norway

1050
Printing invented
Printing, with clay moveable type, is invented in China. Earlier Chinese books were printed using carved wood blocks.

1000
Vikings reach America
Leif Erikson, a Viking explorer, sails to North America, which he calls Vinland.

10th century
Arabic numerals
Arabic numerals (1,2,3 etc) are first used in Europe. Invented in India, they are named after the Arabs who introduced them to Europe.

c.1270
First paper
People in Italy begin to make paper, at first from rags. Paper is much cheaper than parchment, which is made from animal skin.

Maori man from New Zealand

1280
Polynesians settle New Zealand
Polynesian sailors discover and settle New Zealand. After centuries of travel, it is the last place the Polynesians discover in the Pacific Ocean.

1289
First eyeglasses
Eyeglasses are invented in Italy, and are used to help with reading.

1347–1352
Black Death
A terrible plague called the Black Death spreads from Asia across Europe. It kills between a third and two-thirds of the population.

Rat fleas spread the Black Death across Europe.

1337
Hundred Years War begins
Beginning of the Hundred Years War, a series of wars between England and France that went on for over a hundred years.

1315–1317
Great Famine
Cold, wet weather across northern Europe causes the Great Famine. Crops fail, and at least a tenth of the population starves to death.

29

The Vikings

From the 8th to the 11th centuries CE, the Vikings set off from Scandinavia to attack, trade, and settle in new lands. They sailed along the rivers of Russia to the Black Sea, and out into the North Sea and North Atlantic. They settled in the Faroe Islands, Iceland, and Greenland, and became the first Europeans to reach America. In Britain, they conquered an area that the English called the Danelaw.

A rebuilt longhouse in Iceland

Longhouse

A typical Viking home was a longhouse. It had one big shared room with a fire in the middle for warmth, cooking, and light. People slept on benches around the sides. Animals lived in a separate area at one end of the house.

ICELAND

GREENLAND

KEY (890–1050)

Viking homelands
The areas in Scandinavia the Vikings came from.

Gains abroad
The areas that were taken by the Vikings.

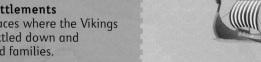 **Viking voyages**
The Vikings went on many voyages in their longships.

Battles and raids
The Vikings fought other people across Europe.

 Settlements
Places where the Vikings settled down and had families.

Eric the Red

Eric the Red founded the first Viking settlement in Greenland in **985 CE**.

Leif Erikson sailed to North America in around **1000 CE**. He named the place he found Vinland.

Leif Erikson

VINLAND

SCALE

0   500 miles

0   500 kilometres

Across the sea

The Vikings sailed all around Europe and the Mediterranean, across Russia, the North Sea, and the North Atlantic.

ATLANTIC OCEAN

The Oseberg Ship

Longships

Voyages were made in double-ended oak ships, with a single square sail. Ships were so important to the Vikings that rulers were buried in them. This beautiful ship was found in a grave in Norway.

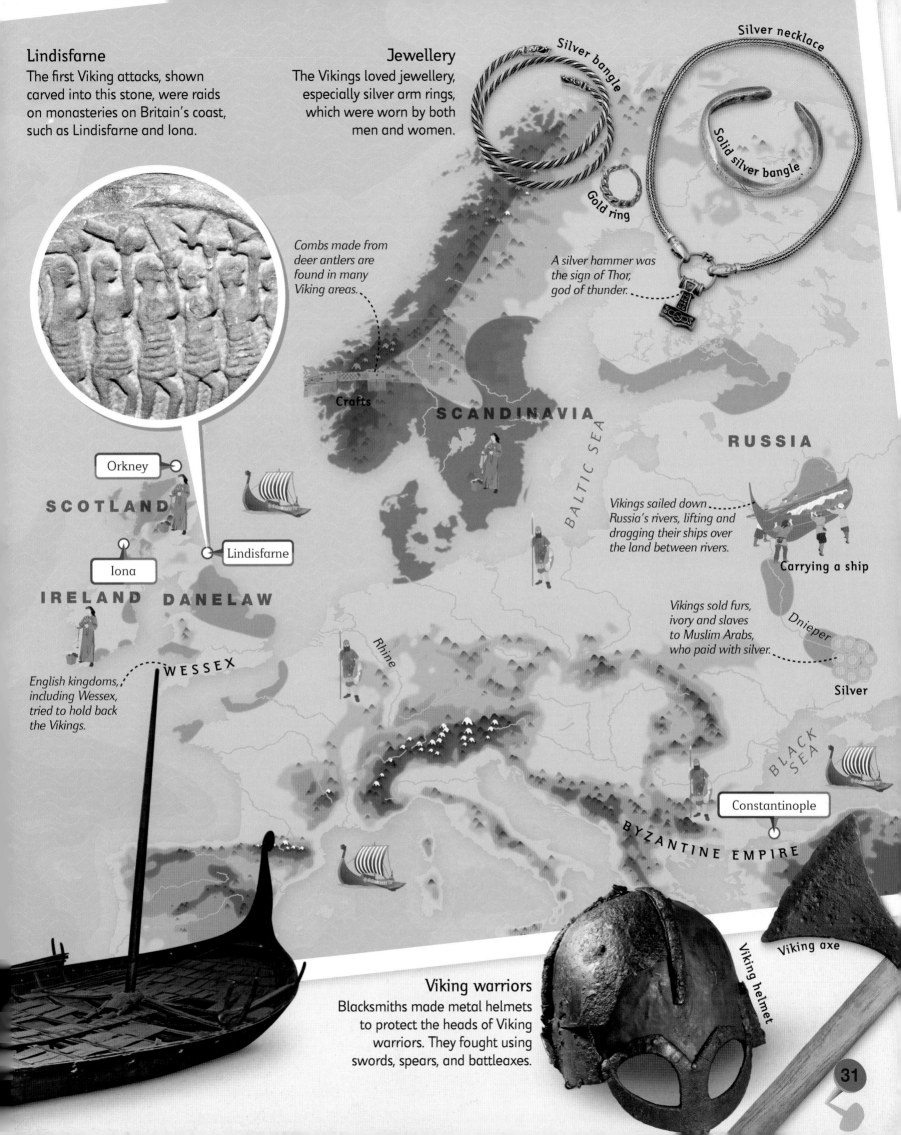

Lindisfarne
The first Viking attacks, shown carved into this stone, were raids on monasteries on Britain's coast, such as Lindisfarne and Iona.

Jewellery
The Vikings loved jewellery, especially silver arm rings, which were worn by both men and women.

Silver bangle

Silver necklace

Solid silver bangle

Gold ring

Combs made from deer antlers are found in many Viking areas.

A silver hammer was the sign of Thor, god of thunder.

Crafts

SCANDINAVIA

BALTIC SEA

RUSSIA

Orkney

SCOTLAND

Vikings sailed down Russia's rivers, lifting and dragging their ships over the land between rivers.

Carrying a ship

Iona

Lindisfarne

IRELAND DANELAW

Vikings sold furs, ivory and slaves to Muslim Arabs, who paid with silver.

Dnieper

English kingdoms, including Wessex, tried to hold back the Vikings.

WESSEX

Rhine

Silver

BLACK SEA

Constantinople

BYZANTINE EMPIRE

Viking helmet

Viking axe

Viking warriors
Blacksmiths made metal helmets to protect the heads of Viking warriors. They fought using swords, spears, and battleaxes.

Bulguksa Temple

Bulguksa Temple

Bulguksa Temple
The kingdom of Silla started following the Buddhist religion in 527 CE. The Bulguksa Temple was built in Gyeongju, the royal capital, in 751–774 CE. Bulguksa means "temple of the land of Buddha".

Coastal kingdoms
Korea is an area of land that sticks out from Asia into the Pacific Ocean. It traded a lot with nearby China.

KEY (500 CE)

Goguryeo sold luxuries such as fur, gold, and silver to China.

Gold

Furs

Goods leaving the empire

Goguryeo
The kingdom that Korea is named after.

Baekje
Known for its statues and jewellery.

Gaya
A small group of independent cities.

Silla
The most powerful Korean kingdom.

Silver

Silla crown
In the Silla capital Gyeongju, kings were buried in tombs covered with mounds of rocks. The tombs contained rich treasures, such as gold crowns decorated with antler or tree shapes.

N W E S

Goguryeo men hunted deer on horseback, using bows.

Pyongyang

Hunter on horseback

YELLOW SEA

SEA OF JAPAN

Baekje sculptors made smiling statues of the Buddha.

Buddha statues

Tomb of king Suro

Gyeongju

Kings of Gaya were buried beneath big mounds of earth.

Gwangju

Ancient Korea

By the 1st century BCE, there were three competing kingdoms in Korea. Goguryeo was a large kingdom in the north, Baekje was in the south-west, and Silla in the south-east. There was also a group of independent cities in the south called Gaya. Silla conquered the other kingdoms in 668 CE, but modern Korea took its name from the kingdom of Goguryeo.

SCALE

0   100 miles

0   100 kilometres

Ancient Japan

Between the 4th and 6th centuries CE, Japan was united from lots of small parts into one country under an emperor. The emperors said they were descended from the goddess of the Sun. Japan used Chinese writing and began to follow Buddhism, which mixed with the local religion of Shinto.

The native people of Hokkaido are called the Ainu.

Ainu people

PACIFIC OCEAN

Hokkaido

God-like emperor
Japan has the world's oldest royal family. It has reigned for at least 1,500 years and continues up to the present day. The emperors were thought to be like gods, so only they could rule the country.

Emperor Kanmu (ruled 781–806 CE)

SEA OF JAPAN

Samurai armour

Samurai warriors wore elaborate suits of armour.

Honshu

The Todai-ji temple in Nara has a 15 m (49 ft) tall statue of the Buddha.

The Japanese traditional religion, Shinto, is based on the worship of spirits called kami.

Shinto shrine

Island state
Japan lies off the east coast of Asia. It is made up of four main islands, called Honshu, Hokkaido, Shikoku, and Kyushu.

Edo

Kinkaku-ji is a famous Buddhist temple built in 1397.

Mount Fuji

Mount Fuji is a holy mountain, worshipped as a Shinto spirit.

Kyoto

Todai-ji buddha

Nara

Kinkaku-ji

Himeji

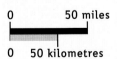
Shikoku

Kyushu

Himeji castle
Wealthy Japanese noblemen lived in castles, where they had their own following of warriors called samurai. This castle in Himeji was originally built in the 1330s.

Inuit hunter carrying a kayak

Inuit
The Inuit, the people of the icy Arctic, lived by catching fish and hunting seals, whales, and walruses. The Inuit chased these animals in light sealskin boats called kayaks.

Homes
People in different areas had different sorts of homes. This photograph, taken in 1876, shows a Paiute village in the Great Basin area. These huts, made from sticks, are called wickiups.

Indigenous people of North America

Before Europeans settled in North America, it was home to hundreds of groups of indigenous (native) people. North America can be divided into ten different regions, called cultural areas. In each area, people shared similar ways of life. In some places, they farmed, while in others they lived by hunting.

The Athabascan people of the Subarctic lived in big log cabins.

BEAUFORT SEA

Log cabin

Athabascan

Inuit

The Inuit lived in igloos, homes made from blocks of snow, which were cosy in winter.

Igloo

In the Northwestern forests, people carved totem poles, decorated with spirit beings and animals.

Chipewyan

Totem pole

The Plains were home to huge herds of buffalo. When the Spanish brought horses to the Americas, people began to hunt buffalo on horseback.

PACIFIC OCEAN

Blackfoot

Chinook

For ceremonies, the Salish people wore headdresses with bird faces.

Salish

Hunting buffalo

Paiute

Crow

Shoshone

Cheyenne

Wikiup shelter

Wickiups were made from sticks. They were easy to build quickly.

Comanche

Apache

N
W · E
S

Varied landscape

North America has many different habitats, with snow in the north and grasslands in the centre. Native peoples lived in all these areas.

BAFFIN BAY

SCALE

0 — 500 miles

0 — 500 kilometres

HUDSON BAY

ATLANTIC OCEAN

In the cold Subarctic, snowshoes helped people cross the soft winter snow.

Snowshoes

Cree

Ojibwa

Mi'kmaq

Iroquois

Huron

In the Eastern woodlands, farmers grew squashes and maize.

Farmers

Sioux

Miami

Huron hair

Huron warriors shaved their heads, leaving hair at the top and back.

War bonnets

Shawnee

Cherokee

Choctaw

Seminole

On the Plains, warriors wore war bonnets made from eagle feathers.

Natchez

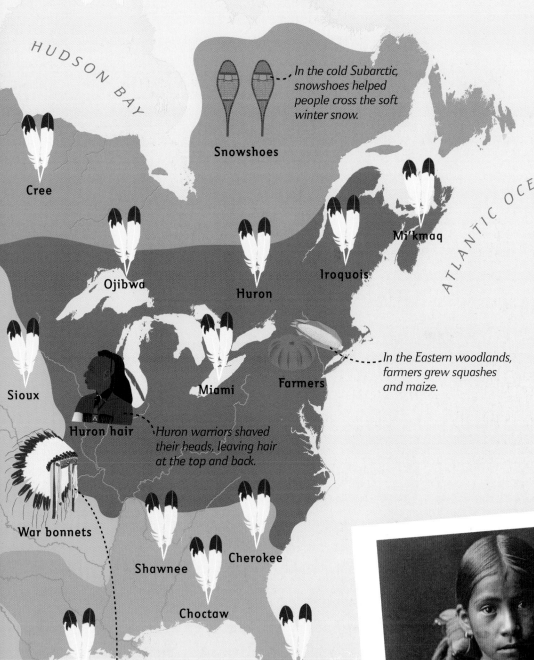

KEY (1500)

 Indigenous peoples
Some of the groups who lived across North America.

Arctic
This is the coldest region, where no trees grow.

Subarctic
Trees grew in the Subarctic, but it was still cold and snowy.

Plains
This region was home to flat, treeless grasslands.

Eastern woodlands
These areas had thick forests.

Southwest
The hottest, driest region.

Southeast
A hot, wet region with forests and swamps.

Great Basin
The Great Basin had mountains, river valleys, and open plains.

Northwest coast
A forested region with mild, wet weather.

Plateau
An area surrounded by high mountain ranges.

California
Home to grasslands, wooded hills, and river valleys.

Apache women

The Apache lived in the hot, dry Southwest. An Apache woman or girl would spend her time gathering wild plants for food, including prickly pears, roots, and seeds. This Apache girl was photographed in 1905.

Apache girl

African empires

Powerful kingdoms have risen and fallen in Africa south of the huge Sahara Desert since around 100 CE. These kingdoms struggled to gain land and control of trade routes. Trading made rulers rich, especially through selling gold, ivory, and slaves. As well as rich monarchs, many ordinary people were farmers in the forests and grasslands below the Sahara.

Timbuktu

The city of Timbuktu in West Africa was famous for being rich. Gold was mined from local gold fields and traded for other goods. Timbuktu was also a centre of learning. There were three mosques where people could study. Sankore Madrassa mosque was built in the 14th century.

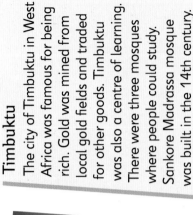

Sankore Madrassa mosque

Islam

North African traders crossed the Sahara Desert on camels to trade with Mali. They brought their religion, Islam, with them. In the 9th century, the people of Mali became Muslims. The Great Mosque of Djenné is the largest mudbrick building in the world.

African powers

The great African empires and kingdoms were to the south of the Sahara Desert, which stretches across North Africa.

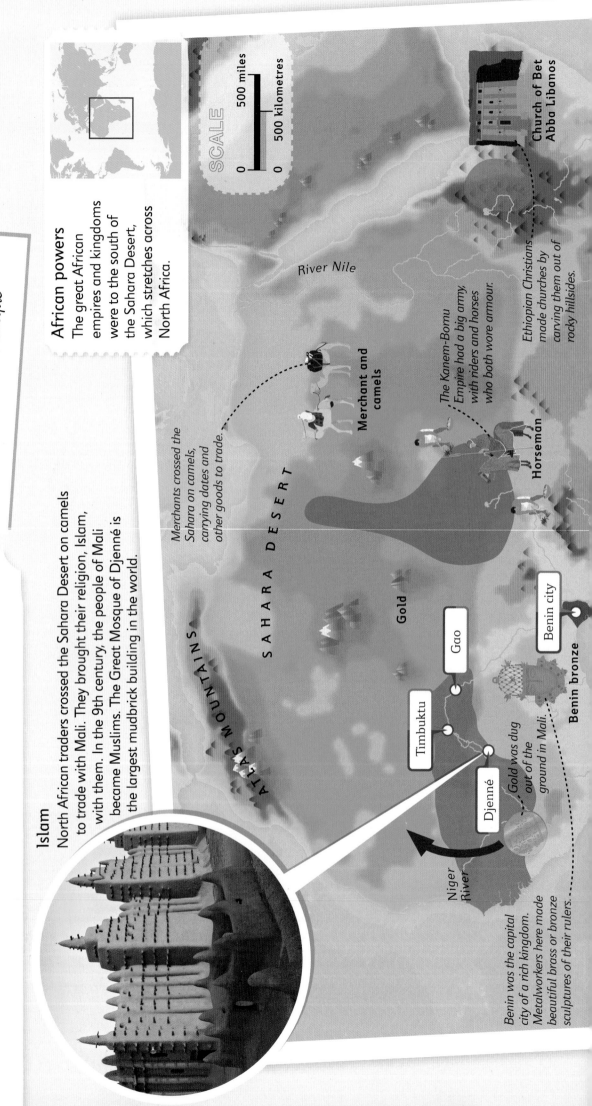

SCALE

0   500 miles

0   500 kilometres

River Nile

Merchant and camels

Merchants crossed the Sahara on camels, carrying dates and other goods to trade.

The Kanem-Bornu Empire had a big army, with riders and horses who both wore armour.

Horseman

Ethiopian Christians made churches by carving them out of rocky hillsides.

Church of Bet Abba Libanos

SAHARA DESERT

Gold

ATLAS MOUNTAINS

Gao

Timbuktu

Benin city

Benin bronze

Gold was dug out of the ground in Mali.

Djenné

Niger River

Benin was the capital city of a rich kingdom. Metalworkers here made beautiful brass or bronze sculptures of their rulers.

King Ezana's Stela

ATLANTIC OCEAN

BASIN

African craftworkers were skilled at making iron tools to trade.

Crafts

INDIAN OCEAN

DRAKENSBERG

KEY (c. 1400)

Trade routes

Mali Empire
This empire lasted from 1230 to 1670.

Kingdom of Zimbabwe
This kingdom lasted from 1220 to 1450.

Kingdom of Benin
This kingdom lasted from 1180 to 1897.

Bunyoro-Kitara Empire
This empire lasted from the 1500s to 1894.

Ethiopian Empire
This empire lasted from 1137 to 1974.

Kingdom of the Kongo
This kingdom lasted from 1390 to 1974.

Kanem-Bornu Empire
This empire lasted from the 800s to 1900.

Farming
Farmers grew vegetables such as yams or grains such as millet.

Great Zimbabwe

These mysterious stone ruins are part of Great Zimbabwe. This city is said to have been home to 18,000 people in the 11th to 15th centuries. Great Zimbabwe grew rich from trading in iron, copper, salt, gold, and ivory (elephant tusk).

Aksum

The earliest African kingdom was Aksum in Ethiopia, which lasted from around 100 CE to 940 CE. Aksum's riches came from trading goods by sea with Egypt and Arabia. Early kings of Aksum built tall stone grave markers, called stelae. King Ezana had this one put up in the 4th century.

King of Kongo

West African kings traded with Europeans, such as the Portuguese, from the 1480s. The kings of Kongo became Christians, and even took Portuguese names. This picture shows King Alvaro meeting Dutch visitors.

King Alvaro of Kongo in 1642

The Silk Road

The trade route that allowed merchants to travel from east to west from Asia to Europe was known as the Silk Road. This road was first set up in around 200 BCE and lasted until sea routes across the Indian Ocean replaced it in the 1500s CE. As well as things to trade, new ideas, religions, and inventions travelled along the Silk Road.

East to west

The Silk Road began in China. It stretched through the mountains and deserts of central Asia to the eastern Mediterranean Sea.

Marco Polo

In 1271 the young Italian Marco Polo travelled along the Silk Road to China with his father and uncle, who were both merchants. He wrote a bestselling account of his travels when he returned home 24 years later.

Marco Polo

Caravanserais

Merchants travelling along the Silk Road stopped off in caravanserais, or inns. Here they could eat and sleep, and let their animals rest.

A historic caravanserai in Lebanon

West to east

Europe sent glassware, silver, gold, and cotton east to China. Horses from the Ferghana valley in central Asia were much valued in China, and travelled along the Silk Road to get there.

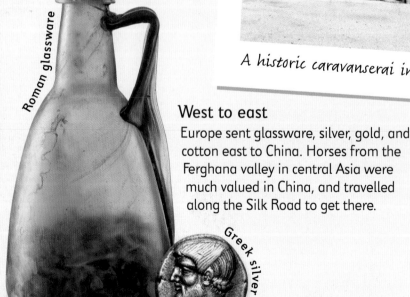

Roman glassware

Greek silver coin

Horses were used to pull carts along, where the roads were good enough.

BLACK SEA

Horses and carts

Roman merchant ship

MEDITERRANEAN SEA

Transporting goods by sea was quicker and cheaper, but also more dangerous.

RED SEA

KEY (220 CE)

Main trade route
This was the path that most travellers and merchants followed on their journeys between east and west.

- Gold
- Silver
- Glassware
- Cotton
- Grapes
- Figs
- Walnuts
- Ferghana horses
- Jade
- Porcelain
- Paper
- Gunpowder
- Tea
- Sugar
- Spices
- Silk
- Salt

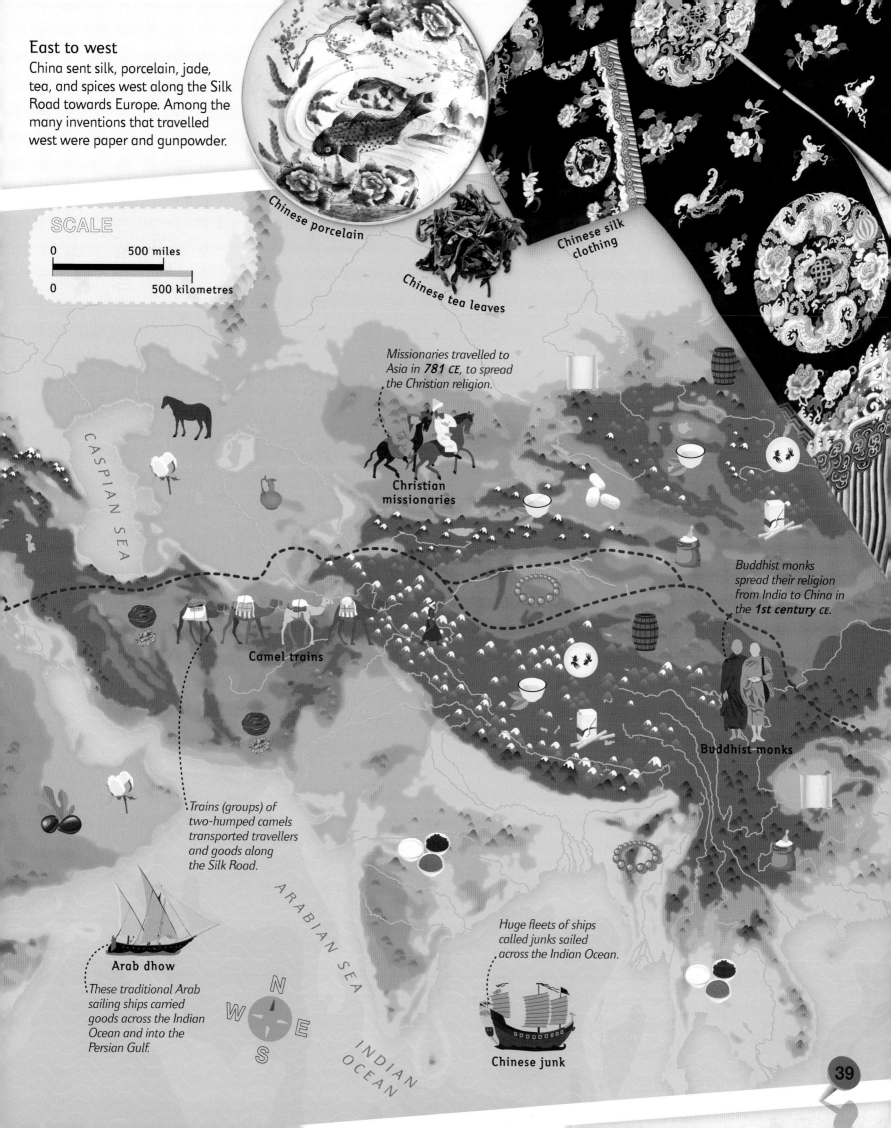

East to west

China sent silk, porcelain, jade, tea, and spices west along the Silk Road towards Europe. Among the many inventions that travelled west were paper and gunpowder.

Chinese porcelain

Chinese tea leaves

Chinese silk clothing

SCALE

0   500 miles

0   500 kilometres

CASPIAN SEA

Missionaries travelled to Asia in **781 CE**, to spread the Christian religion.

Christian missionaries

Buddhist monks spread their religion from India to China in the **1st century** CE.

Camel trains

Buddhist monks

Trains (groups) of two-humped camels transported travellers and goods along the Silk Road.

ARABIAN SEA

Arab dhow

These traditional Arab sailing ships carried goods across the Indian Ocean and into the Persian Gulf.

N
W   E
S

Huge fleets of ships called junks sailed across the Indian Ocean.

Chinese junk

INDIAN OCEAN

39

The Middle Ages

During the Middle Ages, Europe was made up of many kingdoms. This was a period when noblemen lived in castles and fought in wars, riding into battle as knights on horseback. The Christian Church was rich and powerful, building great cathedrals across Europe.

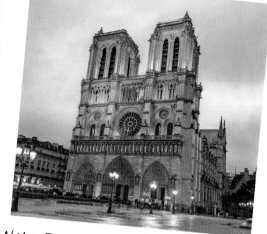

Notre Dame, France, founded in 1163

Cathedrals around Europe

The biggest buildings in Medieval Europe were cathedrals. These were big churches where archbishops based their power. Some cathedrals held the body parts of saints, called relics. People travelled on long journeys, called pilgrimages, to visit these relics.

Stained glass image of Joan of Arc

Joan of Arc

From 1337 to 1453, England and France fought a war, later called the 100 Years' War. Joan of Arc, a peasant girl, helped lead the French to victory.

Canterbury Cathedral contained the bones of the saint Thomas Becket.

SCOTLAND

IRELAND

ENGLAND

Canterbury Cathedral

European castles

Kings and nobles built hundreds of castles across Europe. They used them as bases to fight wars against each other and to rule over the local people.

*France and England fought for over 100 years in this war, from **1337 to 1453**.*

100 Years' War

ATLANTIC OCEAN

FRANCE

Avignon

N E S W

PORTUGAL

ARAGON

CASTILE

EMIRATE OF GRANADA

Castle Hohenzollern in Germany

Power struggles

The countries of medieval Europe fought over land, but shared a strong belief in the Christian religion.

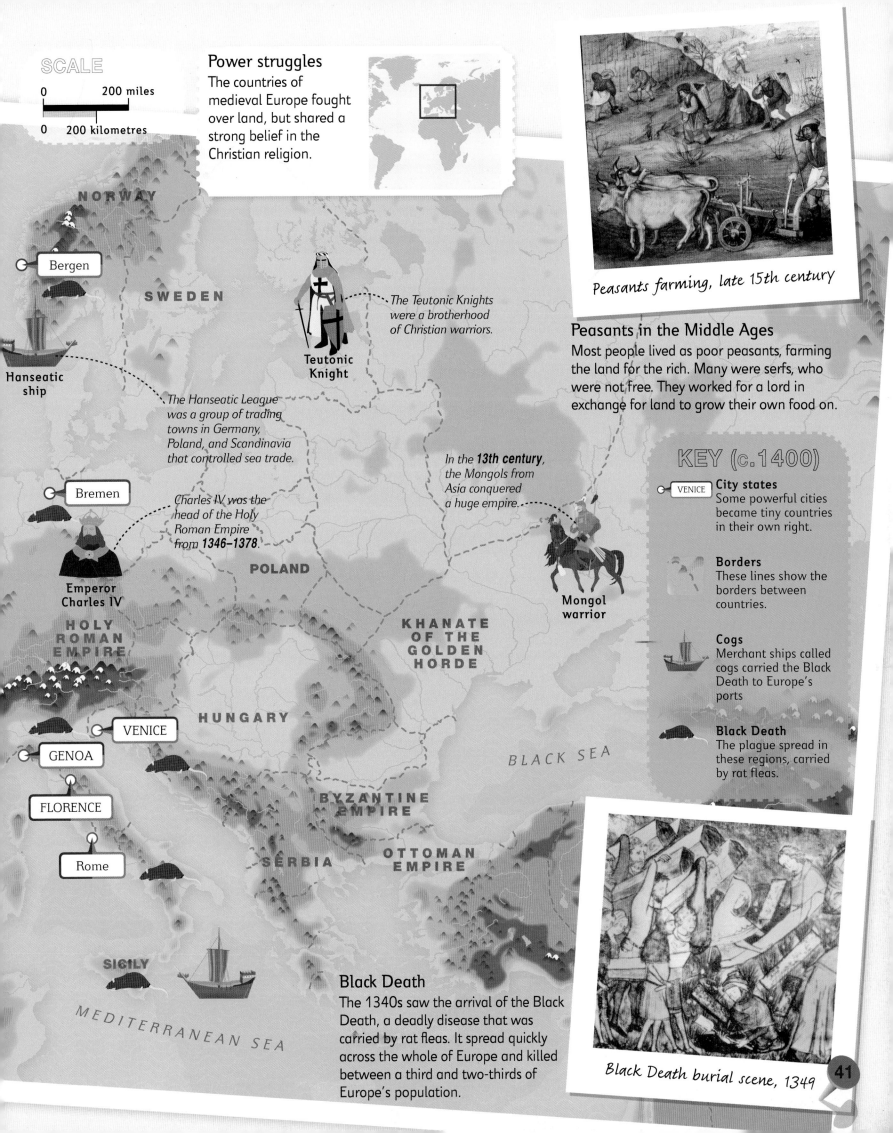

Peasants farming, late 15th century

Peasants in the Middle Ages

Most people lived as poor peasants, farming the land for the rich. Many were serfs, who were not free. They worked for a lord in exchange for land to grow their own food on.

SCALE

0 — 200 miles

0 — 200 kilometres

NORWAY

Bergen

SWEDEN

Hanseatic ship

The Teutonic Knights were a brotherhood of Christian warriors.

Teutonic Knight

The Hanseatic League was a group of trading towns in Germany, Poland, and Scandinavia that controlled sea trade.

Bremen

Charles IV was the head of the Holy Roman Empire from 1346–1378.

Emperor Charles IV

HOLY ROMAN EMPIRE

POLAND

*In the **13th century**, the Mongols from Asia conquered a huge empire.*

Mongol warrior

KHANATE OF THE GOLDEN HORDE

HUNGARY

VENICE

GENOA

FLORENCE

Rome

BLACK SEA

BYZANTINE EMPIRE

SERBIA

OTTOMAN EMPIRE

SICILY

MEDITERRANEAN SEA

KEY (c.1400)

City states
VENICE
Some powerful cities became tiny countries in their own right.

Borders
These lines show the borders between countries.

Cogs
Merchant ships called cogs carried the Black Death to Europe's ports

Black Death
The plague spread in these regions, carried by rat fleas.

Black Death

The 1340s saw the arrival of the Black Death, a deadly disease that was carried by rat fleas. It spread quickly across the whole of Europe and killed between a third and two-thirds of Europe's population.

Black Death burial scene, 1349

41

You can find all the answers and more quizzes on pages 90-91.

8. How many slaves did Europeans capture and take across the Atlantic?

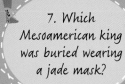

7. Which Mesoamerican king was buried wearing a jade mask?

THE AGE OF DISCOVERY

1450-1750

From the 1450s, Europeans began to explore the world by ship. They conquered the great civilizations of the Americas and captured African people to sell as slaves. New scientific ideas arose, and art flourished around the world.

6. Where is the highest gateway in the world?

5. What is the name of the pyramid at the centre of Chichen Itza?

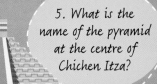

Age of Discovery

From the 1450s, big changes were taking place that brought the Middle Ages to an end. European ships set off on voyages of exploration, which took them all around the world. There were scientific discoveries and new ideas, which were shared across the continent in printed books. Europeans now became the most powerful people in the world. Yet they were divided among themselves because of religious differences.

1452
Portuguese enslave Africans
The Portuguese begin to use African slave labour in their sugar plantations in Madeira.

1497–1498
Portuguese reach India
The Portuguese explorer Vasco da Gama sails to India and back.

Vasco da Gama's ship

The Incas used llamas to carry things for them.

1525
Inca Empire
The Inca Empire of Peru is at its height.

1520–1566
Suleiman the Magnificent
Reign of Suleiman the Magnificent, the most famous Ottoman sultan.

1519–1522
World voyage
Ferdinand Magellan leads a Spanish expedition in the first crossing of the Pacific. One of his ships sails on to make the first voyage around the world.

1529
Siege of Vienna
Suleiman the Magnificent lays siege to Vienna, capital of Austria, but is not able to capture the city. The Ottoman advance into Europe is stopped.

1532
Conquest of the Incas
Spaniards, led by Francisco Pizarro, conquer the South American Inca Empire.

1534
Church of England founded
In England King Henry VIII argues with the Pope and calls himself head of the new Church of England.

King Henry VIII

1631–1648
Taj Mahal
The Mughal Emperor Shah Jahan builds the Taj Mahal, in memory of his favourite wife, Mumtaz Mahal.

Taj Mahal

1619
African slaves in North America
The first African slaves are brought to North America by the English.

1453
Ottomans capture Constantinople
Ottoman Turks capture Constantinople, rename it Istanbul, and make it their capital.

A book printed by Gutenberg

1455
First European printed book
Johannes Gutenberg, inventor of the printing press, creates the first printed book in Europe. The invention spreads and by 1500, 20 million books have been printed.

1488
Portuguese sail around Africa
The Portuguese explorer Bartolomeu Dias sails around the southern tip of Africa, which he names the "Cape of Good Hope". Europeans can now sail to India.

1497
English reach Newfoundland
John Cabot, an Italian, leads an English voyage to Newfoundland in North America.

1493
Spanish found Hispaniola
Columbus founds the first European settlement in the Americas, La Isabela on Hispaniola in the Caribbean.

Christopher Columbus

1492
Columbus reaches the Americas
The Italian Christopher Columbus sails from Spain across the Atlantic and reaches the Americas, which Europeans did not know about before.

1500
Portuguese reach Brazil
Pedro Cabral leads a fleet from Portugal to India and reaches Brazil, which he claims for Portugal.

1501–1504
Michelangelo's *David*
In Florence, the Italian artist Michelangelo carves his famous sculpture of *David*.

1510
Transatlantic slave trade
The Spanish take 50 African slaves to Hispaniola, beginning the transatlantic slave trade.

1519–1521
Spaniards conquer the Aztecs
A group of Spaniards led by Hernan Cortes conquer the Aztec Empire of Mexico.

1517
The Church divides
In Germany, Martin Luther challenges the teachings of the Church, leading to a later split between Protestants and Catholics.

1516–1517
Rise of the Ottoman Empire
Ottoman Turks conquer Arabia, Syria, and Egypt.

1534–1542
French reach Canada
The French explorer Jacques Cartier makes three voyages to Canada, which he claims for France.

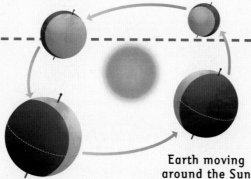

Earth moving around the Sun

1543
Copernicus says the Earth moves around the Sun
Polish astronomer Nicolas Copernicus argues that the Earth goes around the Sun rather than the other way round.

1609–1616
Blue Mosque
The Ottoman sultan, Ahmed I, builds the Blue Mosque in Istanbul.

1607
English settle in North America
The English found Jamestown in Virginia, beginning their settlement of North America.

1588
Spanish Armada defeated
During a war with Protestant England, Catholic Spain sends an Armada (fleet of ships) to invade England, but it is defeated.

Queen Elizabeth I of England

Aztec and Maya civilizations

Mesoamerica (middle America) was home to the Maya, who lived in many cities, ruled by kings who fought each other. Their civilization was at its height between 300 and 900 CE. Later, in the 16th century, the Aztecs of Mexico conquered a great empire. Both peoples built cities with tall, pyramid-shaped temples.

Carved Maya writing

Writing
The Maya were the only American people to invent a complete writing system, with signs standing for sounds and ideas. Maya writing was carved onto monuments and written in books made of fig tree bark.

GULF OF MEXICO

N
W E
S

Tlacopan

Tenochtitlan

Tetzcoco

Cholula

Aztec warriors wore colourful costumes, dressing as eagles and jaguars.

The Olmecs, an earlier civilization, carved huge stone heads from **900 BCE**.

Chichen Itza

El Castillo

A stepped pyramid, El Castillo, is at the centre of the Maya city of Chichen Itza, built around **600 CE**.

At their great temple in Tenochtitlan, the Aztecs killed prisoners as sacrifices (offerings) to the gods.

Great temple at Tenochtitlan

Aztec warrior

Olmec heads

Palenque

Bonompak

Yaxchilan

Tikal

Copan

Tehuantepec

Maya kings were seen as living gods. King Pacal of Palenque was buried beneath a pyramid-shaped temple, wearing a jade mask.

Maya king

KEY

Aztec Empire
The greatest extent of the Aztec Empire.

Maya region
The area under the influence of Maya cities.

Goods coming in
Conquered people had to send gifts to their Aztec rulers.

Cocoa
Cocoa beans were used to make a hot chocolate drink.

Feathers
Colourful feathers were of great value.

Between continents
The Aztecs and Maya lived in Mesoamerica, which lies in the middle of North and South America. "Meso" means "middle".

PACIFIC OCEAN

SCALE
0   100 miles

0   100 kilometres

Emperor Atahualpa

Inca emperor

The emperor, called the Sapa Inca, said he was descended from the Sun god. He was seen as a living god. When Inca emperors died, their bodies were preserved as mummies.

Inca terraces

The Incas conquered the Chimu people in the 1470s. They were skilled at working in gold.

Chimu gold

Chan Chan

Nazca people made huge drawings in the desert.

Nazca carvings

Nazca

Machu Picchu

Cuzco

Cuzco walls

Lake Titicaca

Ruins of Machu Picchu

The town of Machu Picchu was built 2.7 km (1.6 miles) above sea level, high in the Andes mountains.

Inca walls used huge blocks, carved into different shapes, which fitted tightly together.

PACIFIC OCEAN

Terraces

The Incas solved the problem of growing food on steep mountainsides by building flat, raised strips of earth called terraces. They grew potatoes, quinoa, and other crops.

Llamas were kept for wool, meat, dung (which was burned as fuel), and to carry loads.

Llamas

The Inca improved old roads and built new ones to make a network 39,900 km (24,800 miles) long.

N W E S

SCALE

0 ——— 250 miles

0 ——— 250 kilometres

Inca Empire

The 16th-century Inca Empire, in the high Andes mountains of Peru, was the biggest and best organized in America. The emperor was at the top of Inca society. Under him were thousands of officials, then millions of ordinary people who worked as farmers, soldiers, and builders.

High empire

The Inca Empire ran for 4,000 km (2,500 miles) down the west coast of South America. Much of it was high up in the Andes mountain range.

Voyages of discovery

In the 15th century, an age of discovery began, with explorers setting off on long sea journeys. The earliest voyages were made by the Chinese in the early 1400s. Later, European explorers, searching for a new sea route to Asia, found America instead.

John Cabot sailed the Matthew to North America.

John Cabot, like Columbus, hoped to get to Asia by sailing west in 1497.

ARCTIC OCEAN

ENGLAND

The *Matthew*

John Cabot

SPAIN

PORTUGAL

KEY

➤ Zheng He's seven voyages, 1405–1433.

➤ Christopher Columbus's voyage, 1492.

➤ Vasco da Gama's voyage, 1497–1498.

➤ John Cabot's voyage, 1497.

➤ Ferdinand Magellan's voyage, 1519–1521.

Hoping to reach Asia, Columbus sailed the Santa Maria to the Caribbean.

NORTH AMERICA

The *Santa Maria*

ATLANTIC OCEAN

Mapping the world

This map shows what Europeans thought the world looked like in 1491. Europe is on the left and Asia is on the right. There is no America because Europeans had not discovered it yet.

15th-century map

SOUTH AMERICA

São Gabriel

Vasco da Gama sailed to India and back in the São Gabriel.

PACIFIC OCEAN

SOUTHERN OCEAN

48

In *1497*, Vasco da Gama sailed from Portugal to India.

Christopher Columbus sailed from Spain to the Caribbean in *1492*.

In *1519*, Ferdinand Magellan sailed from Spain to the Pacific.

Vasco da Gama

Christopher Columbus

Ferdinand Magellan

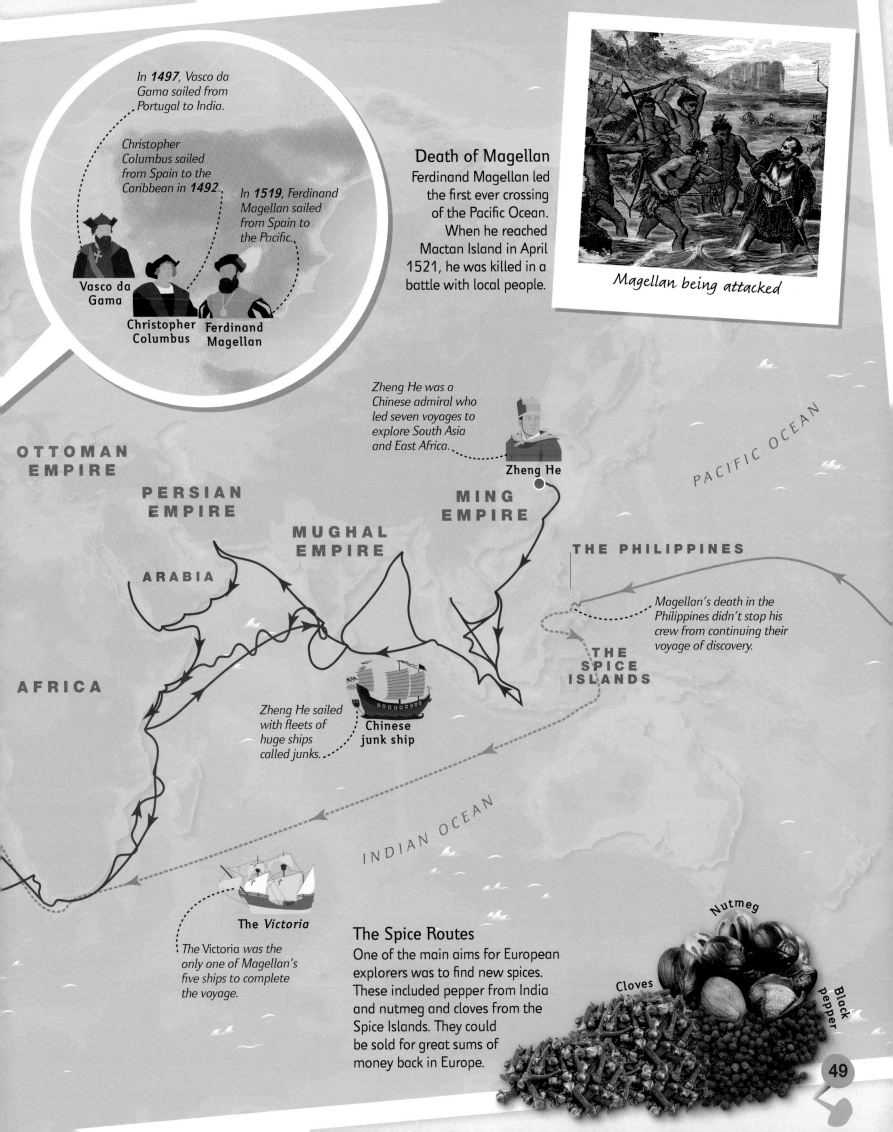

Death of Magellan

Ferdinand Magellan led the first ever crossing of the Pacific Ocean. When he reached Mactan Island in April 1521, he was killed in a battle with local people.

Magellan being attacked

Zheng He was a Chinese admiral who led seven voyages to explore South Asia and East Africa.

Zheng He

PACIFIC OCEAN

OTTOMAN EMPIRE

PERSIAN EMPIRE

MUGHAL EMPIRE

ARABIA

MING EMPIRE

THE PHILIPPINES

Magellan's death in the Philippines didn't stop his crew from continuing their voyage of discovery.

THE SPICE ISLANDS

AFRICA

Zheng He sailed with fleets of huge ships called junks.

Chinese junk ship

The *Victoria*

The Victoria was the only one of Magellan's five ships to complete the voyage.

INDIAN OCEAN

The Spice Routes

One of the main aims for European explorers was to find new spices. These included pepper from India and nutmeg and cloves from the Spice Islands. They could be sold for great sums of money back in Europe.

Nutmeg

Cloves

Black pepper

49

The Mughal Empire

In the 1520s, a ruler from Central Asia called Babur invaded India. His empire made breakthroughs in science, such as new star-gazing technology. The Mughals ruled most of India before it was taken over by Britain in 1857.

Babur in a scene from the Baburnama

Mughal founder

Babur had conquered and lost lands in Central Asia before he successfully founded the Mughal Empire. He wrote a book about his life called the *Baburnama*, which described his military conquests.

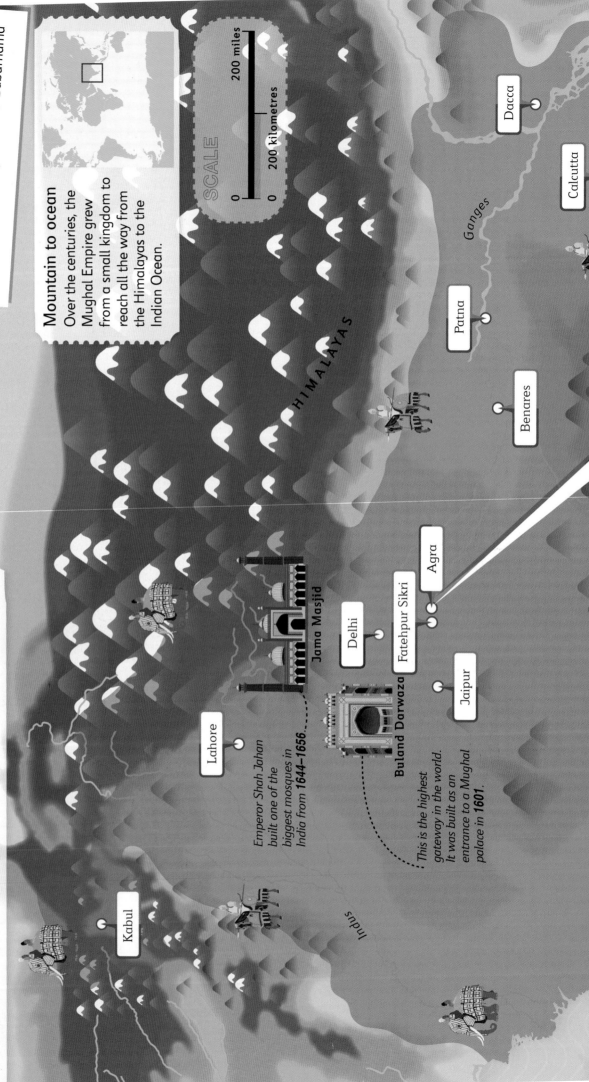

Mountain to ocean

Over the centuries, the Mughal Empire grew from a small kingdom to reach all the way from the Himalayas to the Indian Ocean.

SCALE

0 — 200 miles

0 — 200 kilometres

Dacca

Calcutta

Ganges

Patna

Benares

HIMALAYAS

Jama Masjid

Emperor Shah Jahan built one of the biggest mosques in India from 1644–1656.

Delhi

Agra

Fatehpur Sikri

Buland Darwaza

This is the highest gateway in the world. It was built as an entrance to a Mughal palace in 1601.

Jaipur

Lahore

Kabul

Indus

Taj Mahal

The Taj Mahal – which means "crown of the palace" – was built by Mughal Emperor Shah Jahan (1628–1658) to hold the tomb of his favourite wife, Mumtaz Mahal. Mughal buildings often had onion-shaped domes.

Turmeric

Cinnamon

Ginger

Cardamom

Europeans in India

In 1498, Portuguese explorer Vasco da Gama sailed to India, which was little known in Europe. The spices he brought back encouraged many more Europeans to travel to India.

BAY OF BENGAL

CEYLON

Madras

Pondicherry

Cochin

Calicut

Rise and fall

The empire reached its largest size under the sixth Mughal emperor, Aurangzeb (1658–1707). He took over many lands and ruled over 160 million people. These lands were lost after his death.

INDIA

Goa

Bombay

Surat

ARABIAN SEA

Portuguese ship

The Portuguese were the first Europeans to sail to India. Other Europeans followed.

Dhow

Arab and Indian traders crossed the seas in ships called dhows, which had large triangular sails.

KEY (c. 1700)

Akbar's empire
Akbar (1556–1605) made Babur's empire bigger by conquering many lands.

Southern conquests
Southern India was conquered by Emperor Aurangzeb between the 1650s and 1680s.

Mughal armies
Mughal warriors fought battles to gain land or defend the empire.

Mughal war elephant
Elephants were used in Mughal battles.

Aurangzeb as a young man

The Ottoman Empire

Between 1300 and 1699, the Ottoman Turks conquered a vast empire, which stretched from North Africa to the Indian Ocean. At its largest, more than 35 million people lived under Ottoman rulers, called sultans.

KEY (c.1566)

Goods coming into empire

Furs
Luxurious furs were bought from icy Russia.

Slaves
Slaves did many jobs, from paperwork to guarding the sultan.

Spices
Used to flavour food.

Incense
Burning incense released perfume.

Silk
Raw silk was made into fine cloth.

Belgrade

TYRRHENIAN SEA

N W E S

Tunis

Algiers

TUNISIA

ALGERIA

Ottoman galley

Ottoman warships, called galleys, were rowed by prisoners, who were chained to benches.

Tripoli

TRIPOLI

Istanbul

In 1453, the Ottomans conquered Constantinople. It was renamed Istanbul, which means "in the city". Istanbul's Blue Mosque was built by Sultan Ahmed between 1609 and 1616.

Empire founder

The word "Ottoman" comes from the name of the first ruler, Osman I. He founded a small state in northern Anatolia in the early 1300s.

The Blue Mosque

Osman I, ruled 1299–1324

HUNGARY

Janissary

Bucharest

Sofia

Janissary warriors were Christian boys taken as slaves, converted to Islam, and trained to be soldiers.

Istanbul

Plate

Izmir

GREECE

CRETE

BLACK SEA

ANATOLIA

Ottoman craft workers made ceramics decorated with flowers.

CYPRUS

MEDITERRANEAN SEA

SYRIA

Damascus

Baghdad

Jerusalem

Cairo

Woman wearing veil
The women of the Ottoman Empire covered their heads or faces with veils.

Bedouins with camels

Travelling Arabs, called Bedouins, crossed the desert with their camels carrying goods to sell.

EGYPT

RED SEA

PERSIAN GULF

Mecca

Suleiman the Magnificent
The most famous Ottoman ruler was Suleiman the Magnificent. He ruled from 1520 to 1566. He fought battles but also wrote laws to keep the peace.

Coastal empire
The Ottoman Empire spread along the coasts of Europe, North Africa, and the Middle East. It included many cultures.

SCALE

0   250 miles

0   250 kilometres

53

The Renaissance

From the 1400s, there were big advances in art and science in Europe. Artists were inspired by Ancient Greek and Roman works of art, which had been rediscovered. That is why this period is called the Renaissance, meaning "rebirth". New ideas were spread quickly thanks to the invention of the printing press in Germany.

KEY (1430–1530)

Borders
The borders that separated countries.

Printing press
The printing press was used to print books, which spread ideas quickly. Presses were set up in many cities.

SCOTLAND

Martin Luther defending his ideas in 1521

In England, composers wrote music for the lute, a stringed instrument.

Lute

ENGLAND

Erasmus was a famous Renaissance writer and thinker.

Erasmus

Antwerp

London

Ghent

The Church divides
In 1517 Martin Luther, a German priest, challenged many of the teachings of the Catholic Church. As a result, Luther's followers founded new Protestant churches.

Paris

New view of Earth
The Church taught that the Earth was the centre of the Universe. But in the early 1500s, the Polish astronomer Nicolas Copernicus argued that Earth and the other planets moved around the Sun.

Model Universe with Earth at the centre

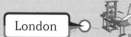

ATLANTIC OCEAN

FRANCE

The astrolabe was used by Portuguese explorers to find their way at sea.

In the **1400s**, Portuguese ships set off to explore the coast of Africa.

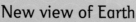
Astrolabe

Madrid

SPAIN

Portuguese ship

Lisbon

PORTUGAL

54

NORWAY

Stockholm

SWEDEN

BALTIC SEA

DENMARK

Copenhagen

HOLY
ROMAN
EMPIRE

Wittenberg

*Dürer was
an influential
German painter
and printmaker.*

Dürer

Mainz

Nuremberg

Worms

HUNGARY

*Venice in Italy was
the most important
trading port in Europe.*

Venice

Genoa

Trading ship

Florence

*In 1436, Filippo
Brunelleschi built a
huge dome for Florence
Cathedral, inspired
by an Ancient
Roman dome.*

Florence
Cathedral

Rome

Pope's
hat

Naples

*The Catholic Church,
headed by the Pope
in Rome, began to
lose its great power
in the Renaissance.*

ITALY

OTTOMAN
EMPIRE

Jan van Eyck

Northern Renaissance
artists, like Jan van Eyck
from the Netherlands,
painted in a new, life-like
style. This portrait of a
married couple skilfully
uses light to make things
look realistic.

Arnolfini portrait, 1434

Michelangelo's David

Ancient Greek sculpture inspired
the Italian artist Michelangelo to
create beautiful new works of art.
In the early 1500s, he carved a
famous statue of David, a hero
from the Bible.

Connected continent

Much of Europe is close
to the sea, and linked
by river. This meant
new ideas could spread
either by water or land.

SCALE

0   200 miles

0   200 kilometres

MEDITERRANEAN SEA

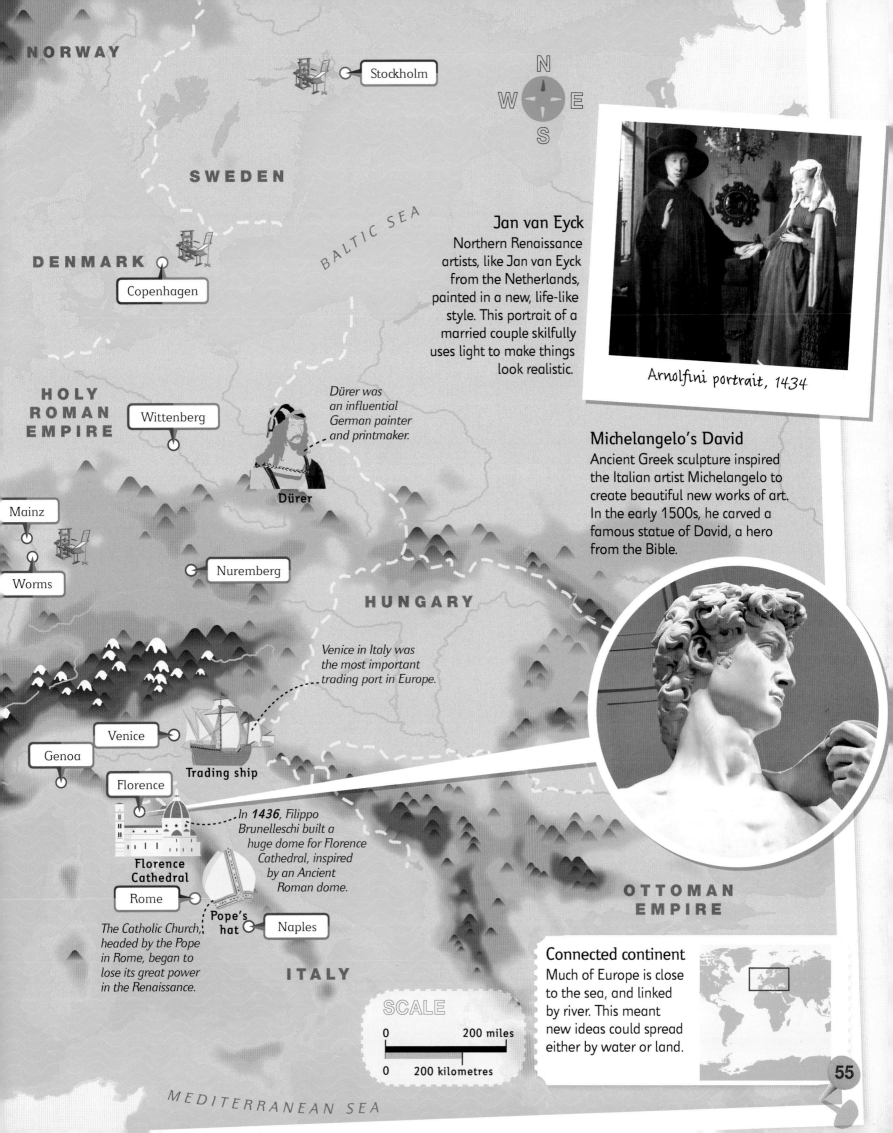

Slave ship

The voyage across the Atlantic was called the Middle Passage. Slaves were kept chained below deck, crammed together so the ship could carry as many people as possible.

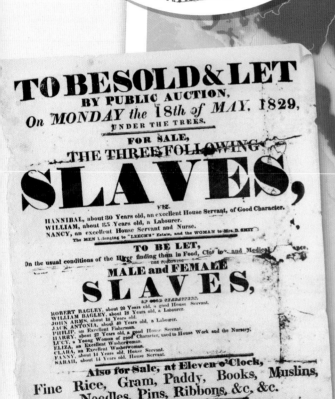

UNITED STATES OF AMERICA

Ships sailed to the US with African slaves to be sold in markets.

Slaves picking cotton

Slaves were forced to pick cotton without being paid.

Slaves

MEXICO

CUBA

JAMAICA

HAITI

Ships sailed from the Caribbean to Europe with sugar and rum.

Sugar and rum

Slave market
In the Americas, slaves were sold at public auctions in port towns. They could be bought and sold again by many different owners.

SURINAME

Slaves worked in gold, silver, and diamond mines in Brazil.

PERU

Gold mines

Diamond mines

Silver mines

BRAZIL

TO BE SOLD & LET

BY PUBLIC AUCTION,

On MONDAY the 18th of MAY, 1829,
UNDER THE TREES.

FOR SALE,

THE THREE FOLLOWING

SLAVES,

VIZ.

HANNIBAL, about 30 Years old, an excellent House Servant, of Good Character.
WILLIAM, about 35 Years old, a Labourer.
NANCY, an excellent House Servant and Nurse.
The MEN belonging to "LEECH'S" Estate, and the WOMAN to Mrs. D. SMIT

TO BE LET,

On the usual conditions of the Hirer finding them in Food, Clothing and Medical assistance,
THE FOLLOWING

MALE and FEMALE

SLAVES,

ROBERT BAGLEY, about 20 Years old, a good House Servant.
WILLIAM BAGLEY, about 18 Years old, a Labourer.
JOHN ARMS, about 18 Years old.
JACK ANTONIA, about 40 Years old.
PHILIP, an Excellent Fisherman.
HARRY, about 27 Years old, a Good House Servant.
LUCY, a Young Woman of good Character, used to House Work and the Nursery.
ELIZA, an Excellent Washerwoman.
CLARA, an Excellent Washerwoman.
FANNY, about 14 Years old, House Servant.
SARAH, about 14 Years old, House Servant.

Also for Sale, at Eleven o'Clock,

Fine Rice, Gram, Paddy, Books, Muslins, Needles, Pins, Ribbons, &c. &c.

AT ONE O'CLOCK, THAT CELEBRATED ENGLISH HORSE,

BLUCHER,

The Slave Trade

Slaves are people treated as property and forced to do work. Slavery was carried out on a huge scale after Europeans settled in the Americas. From the 16th to the 19th centuries, Europeans took 12 million African slaves across the Atlantic. In North America, slaves worked on big farms called plantations.

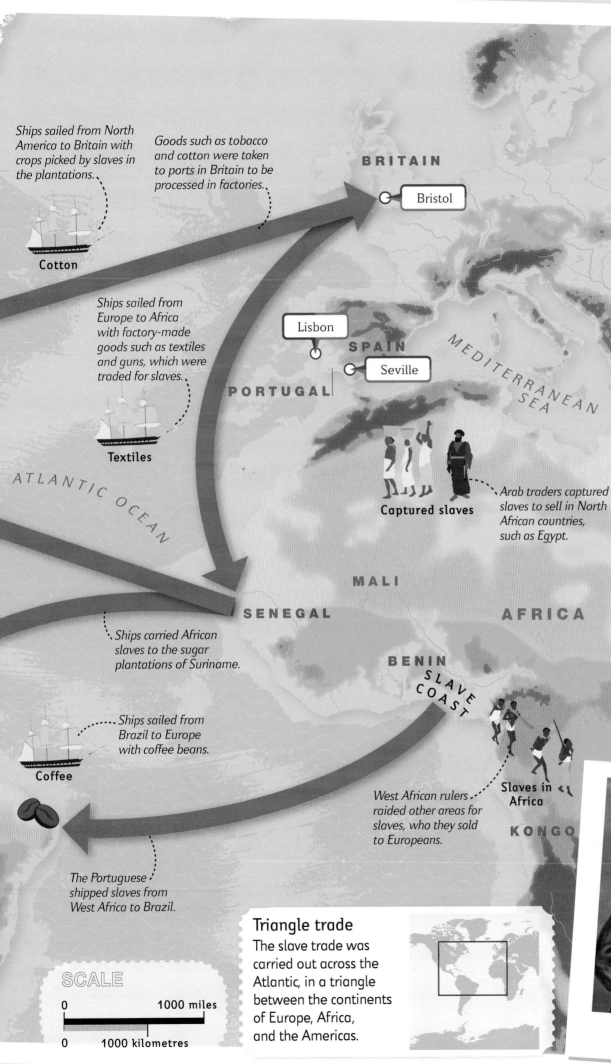

Ships sailed from North America to Britain with crops picked by slaves in the plantations.

Goods such as tobacco and cotton were taken to ports in Britain to be processed in factories.

BRITAIN

Bristol

Cotton

Ships sailed from Europe to Africa with factory-made goods such as textiles and guns, which were traded for slaves.

Lisbon

SPAIN

Seville

PORTUGAL

MEDITERRANEAN SEA

Textiles

ATLANTIC OCEAN

Captured slaves

Arab traders captured slaves to sell in North African countries, such as Egypt.

MALI

SENEGAL

AFRICA

Ships carried African slaves to the sugar plantations of Suriname.

BENIN

SLAVE COAST

Ships sailed from Brazil to Europe with coffee beans.

Coffee

West African rulers raided other areas for slaves, who they sold to Europeans.

Slaves in Africa

KONGO

The Portuguese shipped slaves from West Africa to Brazil.

KEY (c.1740)

Trade route
Slaves and goods were moved on these routes.

Cotton
Fibres of cotton can be woven into cloth.

Tobacco
Dried tobacco leaves for smoking.

Cocoa
The cocoa bean is used to make chocolate.

Coffee
Coffee beans are used to make the hot drink.

Sugar
Sugar was shipped in shapes called loaves.

Ships
Sailing ships carried people and goods across the Atlantic.

Ending slavery

Abolitionists like Sojourner Truth, a former slave, were people who campaigned to end slavery. Britain banned the selling of slaves in 1807, but slavery carried on in the Americas until the late 19th century.

Triangle trade

The slave trade was carried out across the Atlantic, in a triangle between the continents of Europe, Africa, and the Americas.

SCALE

0   1000 miles

0   1000 kilometres

Sojourner Truth

57

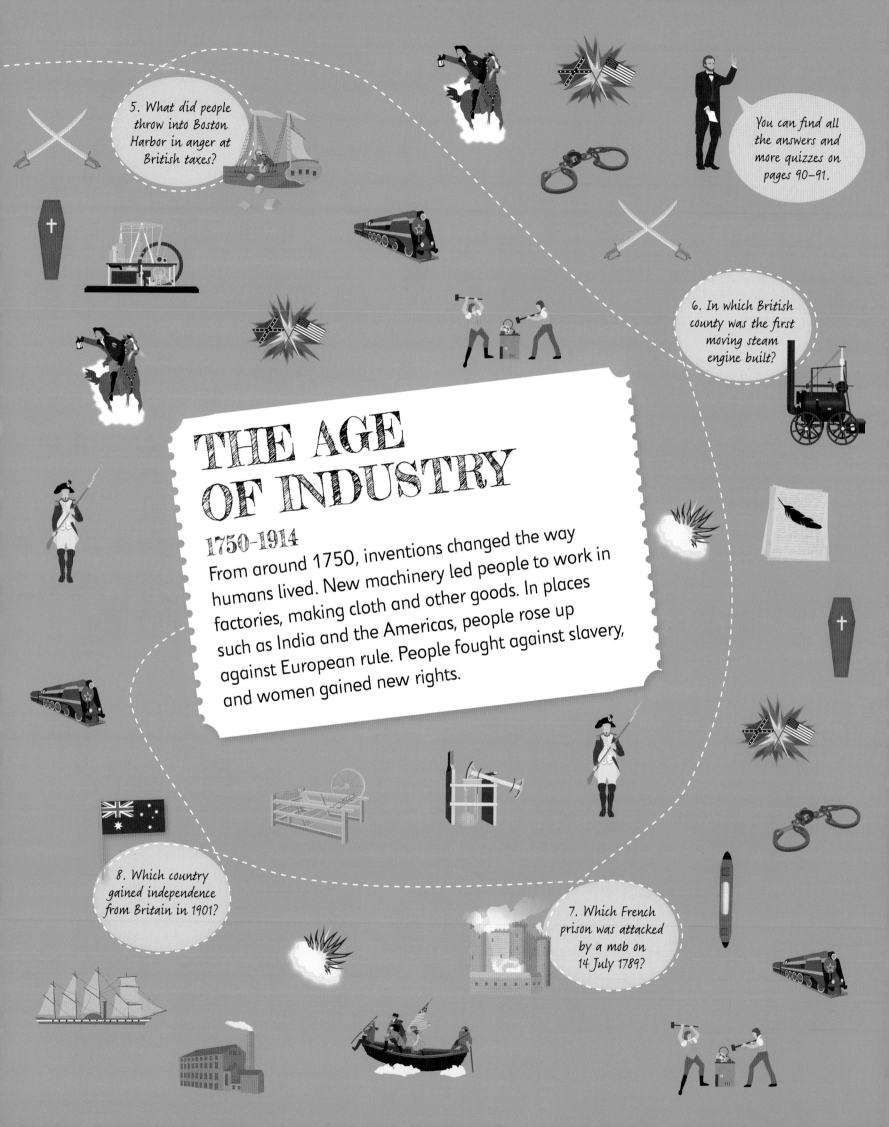

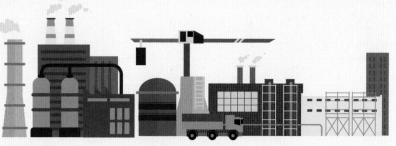

The Age of industry

From around 1750, the world began to change very quickly. People rose up against their rulers, and many countries became independent for the first time. The invention of steam power led to new ways of making things and getting around. This Industrial Revolution completely changed how people lived and worked.

1756–1763
Seven Years' War
At the end of this war, the British Empire grows. It takes land from the French Empire in Canada, America, and India.

1770
James Cook
James Cook makes maps of the eastern coast of Australia, then claims Australia for Britain.

James Cook

1790
Australian revolt
Native Australian people called aborigines begin to fight back against the newly arrived British.

Aboriginal warrior

1791–1804
Haitian revolution
Slave workers on plantations in Haiti revolt, led by Toussaint Louverture. Haiti becomes the first black-ruled state.

1800–1815
Napoleonic Wars
The French ruler, Napoleon, tries to conquer other countries in Europe, and fights wars against other European nations.

1856
Steel
Henry Bessemer invents a process to create steel that is strong enough to make railways, skyscrapers, and machines.

Karl Marx

1848
Communist Manifesto
Karl Marx and Friedrich Engels write and publish *The Communist Manifesto*, describing their radical new ideas about how money should be divided between people.

1839–1842
First Opium War
Britain starts a war against China to force China to trade. In 1842, Britain wins the war and takes Hong Kong.

1857–1858
Indian Mutiny
India tries to become independent from British rule, but does not succeed.

1861–1865
US Civil War
In the US, North and South go to war over slavery and the North wins.

1867
Canadian independence
Canada becomes an independent country and is no longer ruled by Great Britain.

Emperor Meiji

1868
Meiji Restoration
Emperor Meiji takes control of Japan and modernizes how the country is ruled.

1914
Outbreak of WWI
Archduke Franz Ferdinand is shot, which triggers a series of events leading to World War 1.

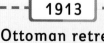

Warship

1913
Ottoman retreat
The Ottoman Empire loses the First Balkan War, and most of its lands in Europe.

1912
Chinese Revolution
Sun Yatsen leads a revolution in China, overthrowing the Manchu dynasty who had ruled for 276 years.

1770
Slave trade
The slave trade reached its peak in the 18th century, with 80,000 slaves brought from west Africa to America every year.

1771
First factory
Richard Arkwright builds the water frame, a spinning machine that is powered by water wheels. His invention is quickly copied.

1775–1783
US independence
The US signs its Declaration of Independence on July 4 1776, breaking free from Britain. The new nation is made of 13 colonies.

1789–1799
French Revolution
People in Paris rebel. They overthrow their King and Queen.

Vive La France!

1776
Steam engine
James Watt develops the first of his many steam engines, and introduces "horsepower" to show how powerful his engines are.

Early steam engine

Napoleon

1803
Denmark bans slavery
Denmark is the first European country to ban slavery.

1811–1828
Independent Americas
Several American countries fight wars against their Spanish rulers, winning independence.

1821–1832
Greek War of Independence
Greece becomes independent, winning its freedom from the Ottoman Empire.

1831
First electrical motor
Michael Faraday, a British physicist and chemist, invents the first electric motor.

Stephenson's *Rocket*

1829
Prize-winning steam engine
George Stephenson designs the *Rocket*, which wins a competition to power the Liverpool & Manchester Railway.

1822
Brazilian independence
Brazil wins its independence from Portugal. Pedro I becomes the founder and first ruler of the empire of Brazil.

First telephone

1876
Telephone invented
Alexander Graham Bell invents the first telephone. People are able to talk over distances for the first time.

1876
Internal combustion engine invented
Nikolaus Otto invents the combustion engine, which can be used to power cars, trucks, and motorcycles.

1893
Votes for women
New Zealand is the first country to give women equal voting rights. The next country to do so will be Australia, in 1903.

1904–1905
Russo-Japanese War
Japan defeats Russia with new, clever tactics and weapons. Japan is seen as a world power for the first time.

Communism grew in Russia after the Russo-Japanese War

1903
First aeroplane
The Wright Brothers successfully fly the first powered aeroplane.

The Wright brothers' plane

Australian flag

1901
Australian independence
Australia becomes independent, and is no longer under British rule.

61

US Revolution

Before the US was a country, there were 13 British colonies in America. In 1775, they rose up against the British, because they wanted to rule themselves. This type of change in government is called a revolution. The colonies fought many battles with the British. In 1783, peace was made and the United States of America became an independent country.

American war
The fighting took place along the East coast of North America. Most of the battles were clustered in the same areas.

SCALE
```
0          100 miles
0   100 kilometres
```

New flag
On 14 June 1777, the Americans flew a new flag. The 13 stars and 13 stripes represented the 13 colonies. Since then, new stars have been added for each new state. There are now 50.

At midnight on **18 April 1775**, Paul Revere rode out to warn people that British troops were coming.

MASSACHUSETTS

NEW HAMPSHIRE

Midnight ride

Boston Tea Party

The colonists won two battles at Saratoga, which gained them support from the French, Dutch, and Spanish.

Saratoga 17 October 1777

Boston

NEW YORK

MASSACHUSETTS

In anger at British taxes on tea sold in America, colonists threw tea into Boston Harbor on **16 December 1773**.

RHODE ISLAND

CONNETICUT

New York

PENNSYLVANIA

Agreed on **4 July 1776**, this document rejected British rule.

Philadelphia

Declaration of Independence

MARYLAND

NEW JERSEY

The British were defeated at the battle of Yorktown. They surrendered, ending the war.

VIRGINIA

Delaware river crossing

On **25 December 1776**, Washington's army crossed the Delaware to surprise and defeat British troops at Trenton.

DELAWARE

Yorktown 19 October 1781

Yorktown

KEY

Important battles
Key fights between the Americans and the British.

NORTH CAROLINA

SOUTH CAROLINA

Camden 16 January 1781

GEORGIA

Charleston 28 June 1776

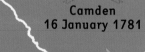

ATLANTIC OCEAN

George Washington
A former farmer, Washington (1732–1799) became leader of the American army in 1775. After the war, he helped set up the new US government and became the first US president in 1789.

George Washington, in 1795

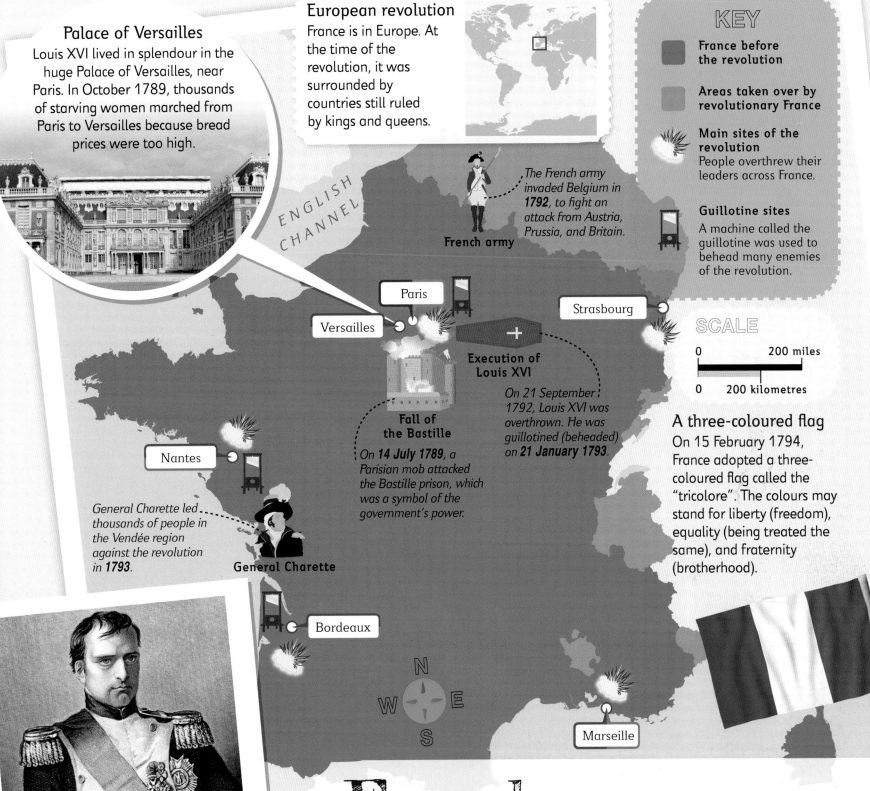

Palace of Versailles
Louis XVI lived in splendour in the huge Palace of Versailles, near Paris. In October 1789, thousands of starving women marched from Paris to Versailles because bread prices were too high.

European revolution
France is in Europe. At the time of the revolution, it was surrounded by countries still ruled by kings and queens.

KEY

France before the revolution

Areas taken over by revolutionary France

Main sites of the revolution
People overthrew their leaders across France.

Guillotine sites
A machine called the guillotine was used to behead many enemies of the revolution.

ENGLISH CHANNEL

The French army invaded Belgium in **1792**, to fight an attack from Austria, Prussia, and Britain.

French army

Paris

Versailles

Strasbourg

Execution of Louis XVI

On 21 September 1792, Louis XVI was overthrown. He was guillotined (beheaded) on 21 January 1793.

SCALE

0   200 miles

0   200 kilometres

Fall of the Bastille
*On **14 July 1789**, a Parisian mob attacked the Bastille prison, which was a symbol of the government's power.*

Nantes

*General Charette led thousands of people in the Vendée region against the revolution in **1793**.*

General Charette

Bordeaux

A three-coloured flag
On 15 February 1794, France adopted a three-coloured flag called the "tricolore". The colours may stand for liberty (freedom), equality (being treated the same), and fraternity (brotherhood).

N W E S

Marseille

Napoleon Bonaparte, in the 1800s

Napoleon Bonaparte
In 1799, a brilliant French army general called Napoleon (1769–1821) overthrew the new government. He crowned himself emperor of France in 1804. Napoleon conquered most of Europe, before being defeated by Britain and Prussia in 1815.

French Revolution

In 1789, many people in France were starving. They rose up against their king, Louis XVI, and his government. In 1792, the French people set up a republic, which meant they could choose how France was ruled. King Louis and thousands of his supporters were killed.

The Industrial Revolution

Britain changed a lot in the 18th century. New machines were invented, and factories opened for the first time, making cloth and other goods in huge amounts. People moved from the countryside to take on factory work in smoky new towns. This period was called the Industrial Revolution.

Industrial towns

New towns sprung up across Britain, housing thousands of workers. Many houses were built back-to-back, with no outside space. Diseases spread quickly in the cramped streets, and living conditions were very bad.

Newcastle upon Tyne, 1877

Cotton factory workers

Factories

Factories were built to contain new machines. Many of the factories made cloth. People who used to make cloth in their own homes now worked long hours inside busy, noisy factories instead.

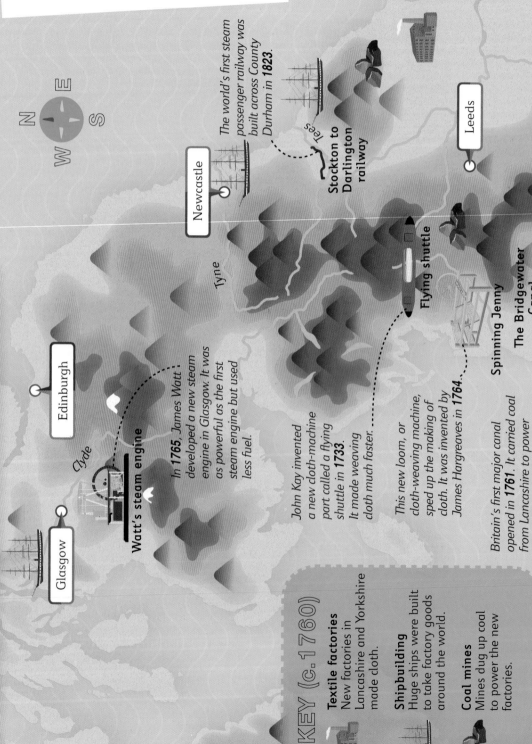

Glasgow

Edinburgh

Clyde

Watt's steam engine

*In **1765**, James Watt developed a new steam engine in Glasgow. It was as powerful as the first steam engine but used less fuel.*

*John Kay invented a new cloth-machine part called a flying shuttle in **1733**. It made weaving cloth much faster.*

*This new loom, or cloth-weaving machine, sped up the making of cloth. It was invented by James Hargreaves in **1764**.*

Spinning Jenny

*Britain's first major canal opened in **1761**. It carried coal from Lancashire to power factories in Manchester.*

The Bridgewater Canal

Flying shuttle

Newcastle

Tyne

*The world's first steam passenger railway was built across County Durham in **1823**.*

Stockton to Darlington railway

Tees

Leeds

Manchester

Liverpool

N E S W

KEY (c. 1760)

Textile factories
New factories in Lancashire and Yorkshire made cloth.

Shipbuilding
Huge ships were built to take factory goods around the world.

Coal mines
Mines dug up coal to power the new factories.

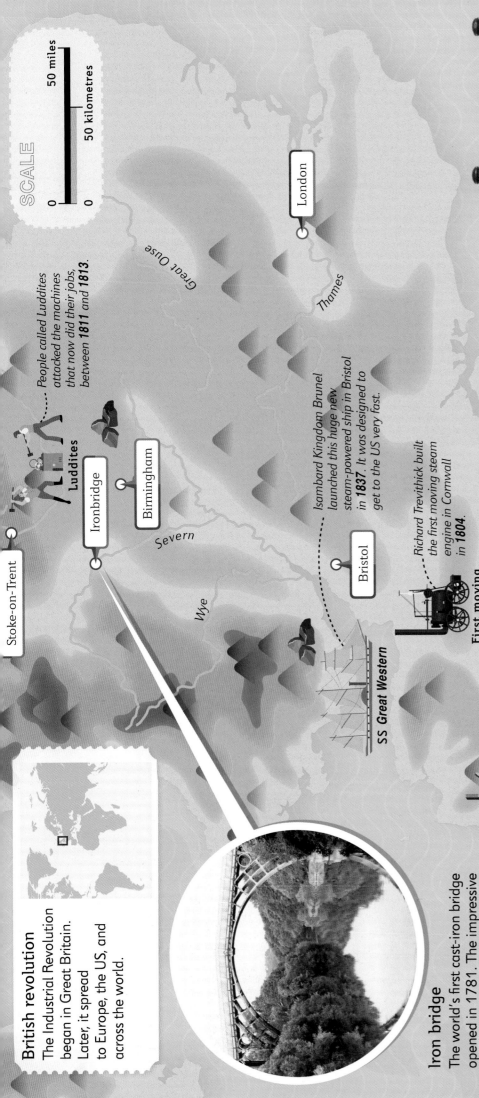

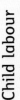

British revolution

The Industrial Revolution began in Great Britain. Later, it spread to Europe, the US, and across the world.

SCALE

```
0          50 miles
0          50 kilometres
```

Stoke-on-Trent

Luddites

People called Luddites attacked the machines that now did their jobs, between 1811 and 1813.

Ironbridge

Birmingham

Severn

Wye

Great Ouse

London

Thames

SS *Great Western*

Isambard Kingdom Brunel launched this huge new steam-powered ship in Bristol in 1837. It was designed to get to the US very fast.

Bristol

Richard Trevithick built the first moving steam engine in Cornwall in 1804.

First moving steam engine

In 1712, Thomas Newcomen built the first steam engine. It pumped water out of mines.

First steam engine

ENGLISH CHANNEL

Cotton-spinning frame

Iron bridge

The world's first cast-iron bridge opened in 1781. The impressive structure crosses the River Severn in Shropshire, in an industrial area now known as Ironbridge.

New inventions

There were many new inventions in the Industrial Revolution. New machines and high-powered steam engines made it faster to create products such as cotton and wool cloth, iron tools, machines, and pottery.

Child labour

Children as young as four worked in the new factories and coal mines. Their work was often dangerous and many were killed. Laws were passed from the 1830s onwards to limit the hours and ages at which children were allowed to work.

A child textile-factory worker

US Civil War

In 1861, a war broke out in the United States that split the country in two. Eleven states feared that the government would free African-American slaves, workers who were owned by other people and not paid. These states left, or seceded from, the United States to form the Confederacy. The states that remained loyal to the United States were known as the Union. The two sides fought for four years.

Abraham Lincoln in 1860

The Confederate flag
When the 11 southern states left the Union and set up the Confederacy, they created their own flag. The 13 stars stood for the Confederate states and the states that supported them.

The Confederate flag

President Lincoln
Abraham Lincoln was elected president of the US in November 1860. He spoke out against slavery, causing 11 southern states to leave the Union. Lincoln led the Union to victory in 1865.

KANSAS

MISSOURI

KEY (1861)

Union states
23 states remained in the Union.

Confederate states
11 slave-owning states left the Union to join the Confederacy.

Slave-owning Union states
Some states stayed in the Union but allowed slavery.

Other states
These states did not get involved in the war.

Cotton fields
Slaves grew cotton on plantations in the South.

Union ships
These blocked other ships from getting in and out of the South. This made it hard to buy and sell things in the Confederacy.

Conflicts
Places where Union and Confederate armies fought.

OKLAHOMA

ARKANSAS

MIS

TEXAS

SCALE

0 —————————— 250 miles

0 —————————— 250 kilometres

Divided country
The US Civil War was fought between the southern Confederate and the northern Union states of the US.

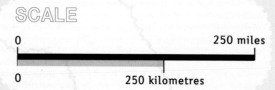

After a long battle, the Confederate fort of Vicksburg surrendered on **4 July 1863**. Its surrender cut the Confederacy in two.

Siege of Vicksburg

LOUISIANA

GULF OF MEXICO

LAKE MICHIGAN

MICHIGAN

NEW YORK

The Gettysburg Address

NEW JERSEY

*In his speech on **19 November 1863**, President Lincoln called the Civil War a struggle for all people to be treated the same way.*

OHIO

PENNSYLVANIA

Assassination of President Lincoln

*On **14 April 1865**, Lincoln was shot by slavery supporter John Wilkes Booth. He died the next day.*

INDIANA

MARYLAND

Washington DC

WEST VIRGINIA

First Battle of Bull Run

*The first major battle of the war was fought on **21 July 1861**. Union troops failed to seize an important railway junction.*

ILLINOIS

KENTUCKY

Richmond

VIRGINIA

Siege of Petersburg

*Union troops won the Confederate towns of Richmond and Petersburg between **9 June 1864** and **25 March 1865**.*

General Lee

*General Robert E. Lee surrendered for the Confederates, ending the war on **9 April 1865**.*

TENNESSEE

NORTH CAROLINA

*Union troops won this big battle on **7 April 1862**. An important Confederate general, Albert Johnson, died in the fight.*

Battle of Shiloh

*The war was started by a Confederate attack on Fort Sumter in Charleston, South Carolina, **12 April 1863**.*

ALABAMA

Capture of Atlanta

GEORGIA

SOUTH CAROLINA

MISSISSIPPI

Fort Sumter, Charleston

ATLANTIC OCEAN

*Union general William Sherman seized the railway city of Atlanta on **2 September 1864**. His troops set parts of the city on fire.*

*General Sherman's Union army destroyed buildings on their way to the coast between **15 November** and **21 December 1864**.*

March to the Sea

FLORIDA

The Freedom Proclamation

On 1 January 1863, President Lincoln ordered all slaves in the Confederacy to be freed. In 1865, the Thirteenth Amendment to the US Constitution freed every slave in the Union.

Newly freed slaves

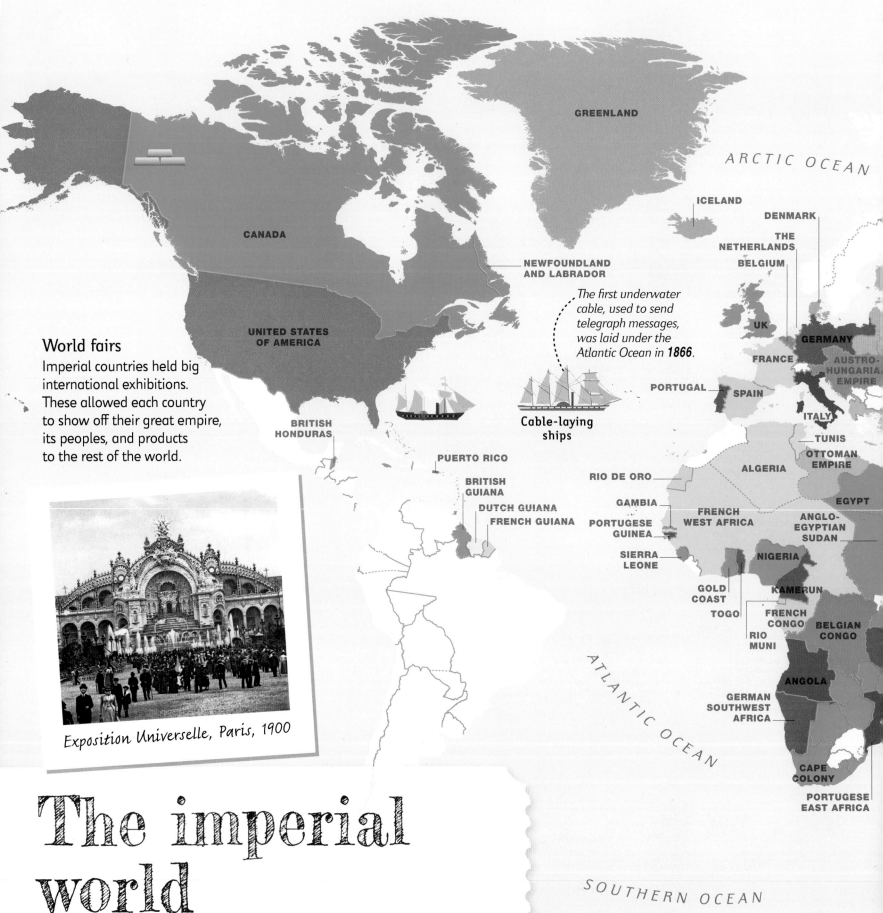

GREENLAND

ARCTIC OCEAN

ICELAND

DENMARK

THE NETHERLANDS

BELGIUM

CANADA

NEWFOUNDLAND
AND LABRADOR

UK

GERMANY

FRANCE

AUSTRO-
HUNGARIA
EMPIRE

PORTUGAL

SPAIN

ITALY

UNITED STATES
OF AMERICA

World fairs

Imperial countries held big
international exhibitions.
These allowed each country
to show off their great empire,
its peoples, and products
to the rest of the world.

*The first underwater
cable, used to send
telegraph messages,
was laid under the
Atlantic Ocean in* **1866**.

**Cable-laying
ships**

TUNIS

OTTOMAN
EMPIRE

BRITISH
HONDURAS

PUERTO RICO

RIO DE ORO

ALGERIA

EGYPT

BRITISH
GUIANA

DUTCH GUIANA

FRENCH GUIANA

GAMBIA

PORTUGESE
GUINEA

FRENCH
WEST AFRICA

ANGLO-
EGYPTIAN
SUDAN

SIERRA
LEONE

NIGERIA

GOLD
COAST

TOGO

KAMERUN

FRENCH
CONGO

BELGIAN
CONGO

RIO
MUNI

ANGOLA

Exposition Universelle, Paris, 1900

GERMAN
SOUTHWEST
AFRICA

ATLANTIC OCEAN

CAPE
COLONY

PORTUGESE
EAST AFRICA

The imperial
world

SOUTHERN OCEAN

By 1900, most of the world was controlled by a few
European nations. The part of the world ruled by each
nation was called its empire. Europeans called the
foreign countries they ruled their colonies.

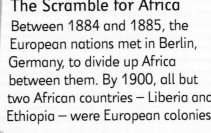

British soldiers in front of the Sphinx in Egypt, 1882

The Scramble for Africa

Between 1884 and 1885, the European nations met in Berlin, Germany, to divide up Africa between them. By 1900, all but two African countries — Liberia and Ethiopia — were European colonies.

A railway that linked together the two ends of the huge Russian Empire was built between 1891 and 1916.

RUSSIAN EMPIRE

Trans-Siberian Railway

PERSIAN EMPIRE

QING EMPIRE

JAPAN

INDIA

Hong Kong

The British Empire gained Hong Kong in 1842 and turned the island into a major business hub.

ERITREA — OMAN

BRITISH SOMALILAND

ITALIAN SOMALILAND

BRITISH EAST AFRICA

GERMAN EAST AFRICA

AGASCAR

FRENCH INDOCHINA

MALAYA

SUMATRA

BORNEO

JAVA

PHILLIPPINE ISLANDS

BRITISH NORTH BORNEO

NEW GUINEA

PAPUA

PACIFIC OCEAN

INDIAN OCEAN

AUSTRALIAN COLONIES

NEW ZEALAND

Queen Victoria

The British Empire

From 1837 to 1901, Queen Victoria ruled the British Empire. By 1900, the empire ruled over 412 million people — almost a quarter of the world's population at the time.

KEY (1900)

- Ottoman Empire
- British Empire
- French Empire
- Danish Empire
- Spanish Empire
- Portuguese Empire
- Dutch Empire
- German Empire
- Russian Empire
- Japanese Empire
- Italian Empire
- American Empire
- Austro-Hungarian Empire
- Belgian Empire
- Persian Empire
- Qing Empire
- Independent nations

Goldfields
People rushed to newly discovered goldfields.

Steam ships
These ships carried emigrants to the US and Canada. They were also used for trading with the colonies.

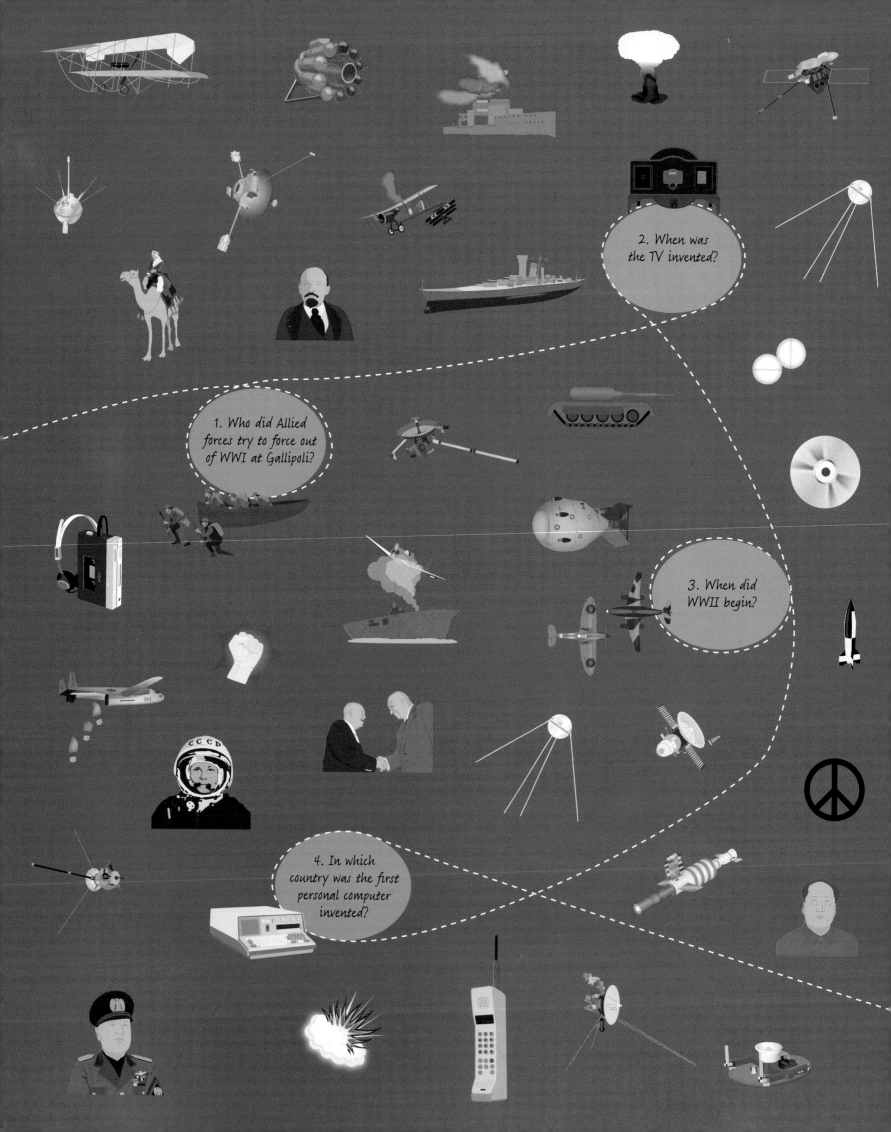

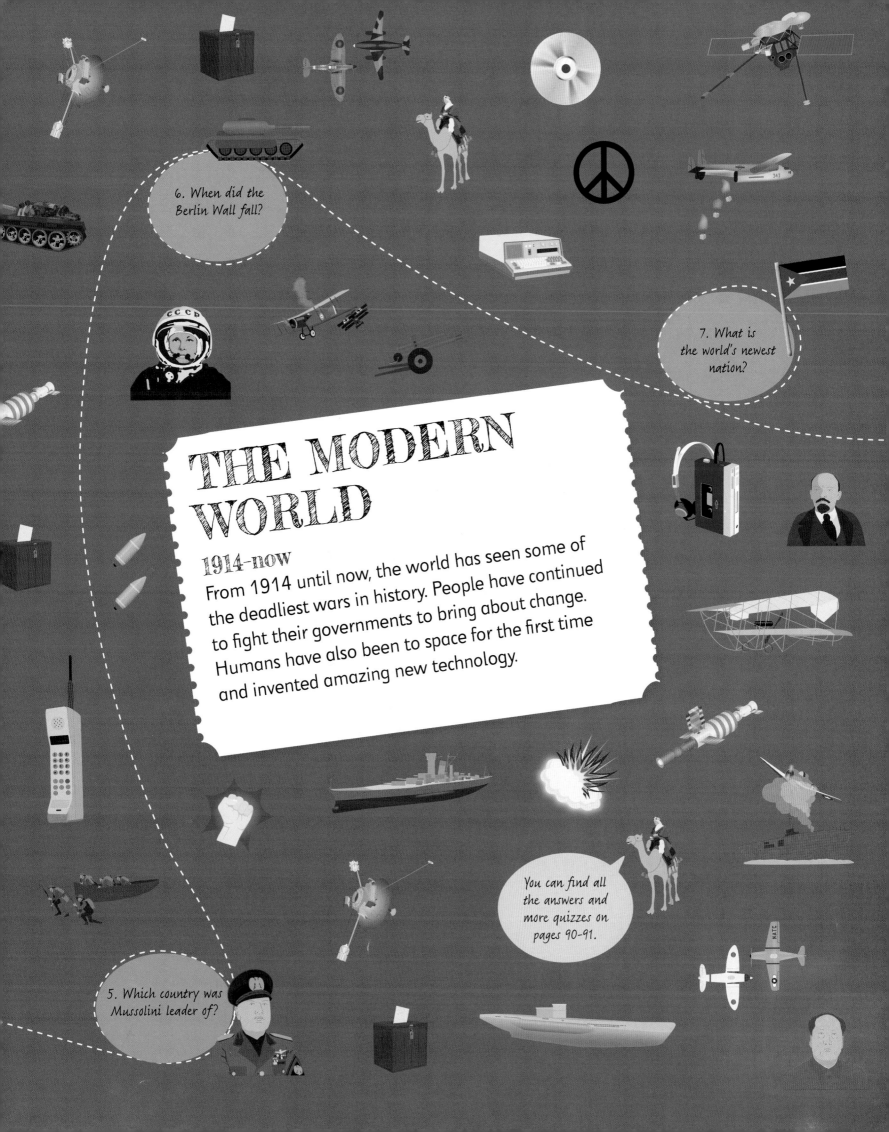

6. When did the Berlin Wall fall?

7. What is the world's newest nation?

THE MODERN WORLD

1914-now

From 1914 until now, the world has seen some of the deadliest wars in history. People have continued to fight their governments to bring about change. Humans have also been to space for the first time and invented amazing new technology.

You can find all the answers and more quizzes on pages 90-91.

5. Which country was Mussolini leader of?

The Modern World

The world today has been shaped by two world wars, huge political changes, and amazing new inventions. People have fought to bring in many different types of government. The population continues to grow and exciting new technology is still being developed.

1914–1918
World War 1
A war that begins in Europe in 1914 is fought around the world for four years. More than 18 million people are killed.

Gas mask used in WW1

1917
Russia in revolt
Russia gets rid of its tsar (king) and becomes the first communist country, aiming for everyone to be equal.

1939–1945
World War II
The biggest war in human history breaks out in Europe in 1939 and soon spreads around the world. More than 60 million people are killed.

1936–1939
Spanish Civil War
The Spanish army led by General Franco fights against the elected government, winning power over the whole of Spain in 1939.

WW2 fighter plane

1957
Ghana gains independence
The Gold Coast becomes the first black, British-ruled colony in Africa to gain independence, becoming the country of Ghana.

Flag of Ghana

1957
EEC founded
Six European nations form the European Economic Community (EEC), making it easier for them to trade (buy and sell) goods with each other.

1953
Everest is conquered
New Zealander Edmund Hillary and Tenzing Norgay from Nepal become the first people to climb Everest, the world's highest mountain.

1957
Sputnik 1 flies around the world
The USSR launches the first satellite made by humans into space. It takes 96.2 minutes to orbit (travel around) the Earth.

1961
JFK becomes US president
At 43, John F. Kennedy becomes the youngest president in US history. He is shot dead in 1963.

John F. Kennedy on a half dollar coin

1962
Cuban missile crisis
The US and USSR almost go to war after the USSR places nuclear missiles on the island of Cuba, close to the US.

1964–1975
Vietnam War
The US fights with South Vietnam against communist North Vietnam. In 1975, North Vietnam wins control of all Vietnam.

2016
Britain votes to leave the EU
A member of the EU since 1973, Britain votes to leave the group.

EU Flag

2012
World population above 7 billion
The total population of the world rises above 7 billion for the first time.

2002
The Euro
Twelve members of a group of countries in Europe called the EU begin using the same money – the Euro.

2001
9/11
Islamic terrorist group al-Qaeda flies two planes into the Twin Towers in New York, US. Almost 3,000 people are killed.

Euro note and coins

1925
Black-and-white TV developed
Scottish engineer John Logie Baird makes the first working black-and-white TV. Colour TV follows in 1928.

Early TV

1928
Penicillin
Scottish scientist Alexander Fleming discovers a new medicine called penicillin. It is used to cure infections and saves many lives.

1929
Great Depression
There is an economic slump from 1929–1939, which means people around the world lose their jobs and don't have enough money.

1933
Nazis come to power
Adolf Hitler's Nazi Party comes to power in Germany. The Nazis soon ban all other political parties – only the Nazi Party is allowed to exist.

Nazi badge

1932
Roosevelt elected US president
Franklin Roosevelt is voted in and promises to create more jobs so that people can earn money.

President Roosevelt

1946
First electronic computer
ENIAC, the world's first electronic computer, is built in the US. It is nicknamed "Great Brain".

Flag of India

1947
India and Pakistan become independent
The British give up rule in India. India and Pakistan become independent. Ceylon (Sri Lanka) and Burma (Myanmar) become independent in 1948.

Flag of Pakistan

1950–1953
Korean War
A war breaks out in Korea as North Korea seeks to take over South Korea. The US fights alongside South Korea.

Tank used in Korean war

1949
China becomes communist
After a lengthy civil war, the Communist Party led by Chairman Mao Zedong takes power in China.

1948
Israel is founded
A new state for Jews is created in the Middle East. Fighting with the Palestinians who lived in the area already turns into a war with neighbouring countries against Israel.

1969
Moon landing
American astronaut Neil Armstrong becomes the first person to walk on the moon.

1973
First PC designed
The world's first personal computer (PC) is designed and developed by IBM in California. It is much smaller than earlier computers.

1982
CDs introduced
Technology companies Philips and Sony produce the first compact disc (CD), to store data such as music.

CDs

1994
Apartheid ends
South Africa ends its policy of apartheid, which treated white and black people differently. Nelson Mandela becomes the new president.

Statue of Nelson Mandela celebrating freedom

1991
USSR breaks up
The Cold War between anti-communist and communist countries ends when the communist USSR collapses. New states are created, including Russia.

1989
Berlin wall falls
As communism ends in Eastern Europe, the Berlin Wall dividing West Berlin and communist East Berlin is pulled down. The city is reunited after 44 years apart.

Inventions

The 20th century was a period of great technological change. The world's first flight, first rocket launch, and first satellite were all in the sky by 1957. Towards the beginning of the 21st century, computers and mobile phones transformed the world. Today, new inventions continue to improve human life.

UNIVAC, an early computer

NORTH AMERICA

*Martin Cooper developed the world's first mobile phone in **1973**. It was the same size as a house brick.*

First hand-held mobile phone

First personal computer

*The world's first personal computer was designed and developed by IBM in California in **1973**.*

First electronic computer

*ENIAC, the world's first electronic computer, was built in Pennsylvania in **1946**.*

First integrated circuit of microchips

*In **1958**, Jack Kilby created a tiny electronic circuit called a microchip. This changed the way technology was powered.*

The computer revolution
The first computers, created in the 1940s, were huge machines that were slow to use. Today's computers are small and can do many different things. Modern computers have changed the way we work, live, learn, and entertain ourselves.

Taking to the skies
Orville Wright was the first person to make a powered flight, above North Carolina in 1903. Thanks to the development of powerful petrol engines, he flew 37 m (120 feet) in 12 seconds on board the *Flyer*.

PACIFIC OCEAN

SOUTH AMERICA

ATLANTIC OCEAN

The Wright Flyer

Philips in the Netherlands and Sony in Japan together developed the CD in **1982**.

The V2 rocket was developed in Germany in **1942**. It was used to bomb cities during WWII.

First compact disc (CD)

First rocket

EUROPE

In **1957**, Sputnik I became the first human-made object to travel around Earth.

First human-made satellite

ASIA

Sony Walkman

The Sony Walkman, developed by Sony in Japan in **1978**, was the world's first portable music player.

In **1942**, Jacques Cousteau of France developed the scuba, letting him breathe underwater.

AFRICA

First airmail service

A plane first carried mail by air in India, in **1911**. More than 6,000 letters were sent this way.

Frank Whittle designed the first jet engine in **1927**.

Alexander Fleming discovered penicillin in **1928**, an antibiotic medicine that kills germs.

First jet engine

First antibiotic

WARWICKSHIRE

London

Black-and-white television was developed by John Logie Baird in **1925**.

First television

In **1959**, the world's first vehicle that could hover above the ground and sea was launched.

First hovercraft

AUSTRALIA

New communications

The world's first telephone voice message was sent by Alexander Graham Bell in 1876. Today's mobile phones are able to send text messages, stream videos, take photographs, and connect to the Internet.

Bell's early telephone

World War I

In June 1914, a war began in Europe that grew to become the First World War. The Central Powers led by Germany fought the Allies – Britain, France, and Russia. Millions of soldiers were killed in deadly battles on land and at sea. The Allies won the war in November 1918.

Franz Ferdinand in 1914

War begins

Austria-Hungary declared war on Serbia after a Serb shot an Austrian prince, Franz Ferdinand, in June 1914. European countries joined the two sides, and war broke out across Europe in August 1914.

NORWAY

Germany and Britain drew at the war's biggest naval battle in 1916.

GREAT BRITAIN

Jutland

DENMARK

German Zeppelin airships dropped bombs on cities in Britain.

NETHERLANDS

GERMANY

London

Ypres, 1915
Passchendaele, 1917

BELGIUM

Pilots fought "dogfights" high above the battlefields.

The Somme, 1916

Paris

Marne, 1914   Verdun, 1916

Dogfights

LUXEMBOU

N
W   E
S

Capor
19

SWITZERLAND

ITALY

Isonzo, 1915–1917

FRANCE

SPAIN

PORTUGAL

Rome

ATLANTIC OCEAN

MOROCCO

TUNISIA

WESTERN SAHARA

ALGERIA

LIBYA

Western Front

The fighting in Western Europe turned into a stalemate, which meant neither side could win. Both sides dug trenches to defend the ground they had gained. Soldiers lived in these muddy trenches, while being fired at by the enemy.

SCALE

0 — 250 miles

0 — 250 kilometres

Two revolutions in Russia in **1917** overthrew the tsar (ruler).

Revolutions in St Petersburg

Moscow

Russia launched deadly attacks against German and Austro-Hungarian forces on the Eastern Front in **1916**.

Tannenberg, 1914

Brusilov offensive

RUSSIA

AUSTRIA-HUNGARY

MONTENEGRO

ROMANIA

BLACK SEA

SERBIA BULGARIA

Constantinople

ALBANIA

Gallipoli

Allied forces tried to force the Ottoman Empire out of the war in **1915**, at Gallipoli.

GREECE

THE OTTOMAN EMPIRE

MEDITERRANEAN SEA

In **1916**, the Arabs rose in revolt against their Ottoman rulers, helped by the British.

Jerusalem

Arab Revolt

EGYPT

Women at war

Women weren't allowed to fight in the war, but they still carried out important jobs. They worked on the land to bring in the crops and in factories to make explosives and bullets for the troops.

KEY

Central Powers
Countries in Central Europe joined together.

Allies
Britain, France, and Russia teamed up as allies.

Neutrals
Countries not in the war were called neutral.

Battle sites
Soldiers fought each other across Europe.

The Allied leaders in June 1919

War ends

In late 1918, most of the Central Powers had stopped fighting. Germany fought on with exhausted troops in Western Europe. A ceasefire ended the war on 11 November 1918, and a peace agreement was signed in June 1919.

Europe at war

Most of the fighting in World War I happened in Europe, though many other countries were affected. The US joined the Allies in 1917.

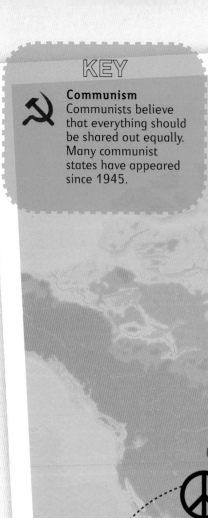
The fascist Nazi Party ruled Germany from **1933** to **1945**, when they lost World War II.

Nazi flag
GERMANY

Eas
Eu
(var

The Spanish Civil War was a conflict between supporters of the fascist General Franco (1892–1975) and believers in democracy. It lasted from **1936** to **1939**.

Spanish **SPAIN**
Civil War **ITALY**

Mussolin

UNITED STATES OF AMERICA

Anti-nuclear movement

Ballot box

People in the US choose their own government by putting votes into boxes. This is called democracy.

People began protesting against governments using deadly nuclear weapons in the **1960s**.

Cuba

Benito Mussolini (1883–194 was the fascist leader of Italy from **1922** to **1943**. He made it illegal to oppose his rule.

ATLANTIC OCEAN

PACIFIC OCEAN

Fascism

Fascists believe in obedience to a powerful leader. The Nazi Party in Germany was a fascist party led by Adolf Hitler (1899–1945). The Nazis believed that Germans were better than all other people.

New ideas

People have often come up with new ideas about society, especially during the early 20th century. Communists believe in rule by a single party, while democrats think that people should have the right to choose their own leaders. Fascists want all-powerful leaders, called dictators. Many people have fought to try to change the way they are governed.

Adolf Hitler at a Nazi event in 1927

Vladimir Lenin (1870–1924) seized power during the Russian Revolution of 1917 and set up the world's first communist state.

Karl Marx in 1875

Joseph Stalin (1878–1953) became leader of communist Russia after 1924 and ruled until his death.

Stalinism

Vladimir Lenin

Russia

UNION OF SOVIET SOCIALIST REPUBLICS

Mongolia

North Korea

China

Mao

More than 70 million Chinese people died from famine or execution during Mao Zedong's rule.

Laos   **Vietnam**

Cambodia

INDIA

INDIAN OCEAN

Green politicians aim to protect the environment. The first Green Party was formed in Australia in 1972.

Green politics

Karl Marx

Karl Marx (1818–1883) was a German political thinker. He thought that people could develop a society in which wealth is owned by the whole community rather than by individuals. This is called communism.

Non-violence

In India, Mahatma Gandhi (1869–1948) wanted to free the country from British rule. He aimed to achieve this change through peaceful activities, such as refusing to buy British goods. Gandhi's work helped force the British out of India in 1947.

Communism in China

The Chinese Communist Party's Mao Zedong (1893–1976) won power in 1949 after a war with other political groups in China. He believed in revolution and got rid of his political opponents. Mao's sayings were collected in the *Little Red Book*.

World War II

In 1939, a war broke out in Europe that spread across the world. Bombs were dropped on cities by planes, and millions of soldiers were killed in battle. Both Germany, led by Adolf Hitler and the Nazi Party, and Japan conquered huge empires. They were defeated in 1945 by a group of countries called the Allies.

Europe and the Far East

The fighting mainly took place in Europe and the Far East, although many other parts of the world were also involved.

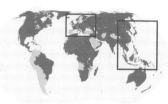

German refugee children in 1938

Children at war

Anti-Jewish laws forced Jewish children in Germany to escape to other countries (become refugees). Other children left their homes in cities to escape bombing.

D-Day

The largest ever invasion from the sea took place on 6 June 1944. American, British, and Canadian troops crossed the English Channel and landed on the French coast to free France from German rule.

German U-boats (submarines) attacked Allied ships in the Atlantic.

*In **1940**, Britain's Royal Air Force beat German planes in a battle in the sky.*

NORWAY

SWEDEN

GREAT BRITAIN

Battle of Britain

ATLANTIC OCEAN

Leningrad 1941–1944

*In June **1941**, the Axis powers almost knocked Russia out of the war with a huge attack.*

Barbarossa

GERMANY

Spitfire

British and American planes regularly bombed German cities.

Blitzkrieg

Kursk, western Russia

Germany took Poland by surprise with a "Blitzkrieg" or lightning war.

POLAND

FRANCE

*German leader Hitler took over France in **1940**.*

ITALY

*Russia won the biggest ever tank battle against Germany at K. between July and August **1943**.*

SPAIN

Monte Cassino, Italy, 1944

TURKEY

Jews in Germany were forced to wear a yellow star with the word "Jude" – German for Jew.

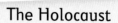

N
W E
S

MEDITERRANEAN SEA

El Alamein, Egypt, 1942

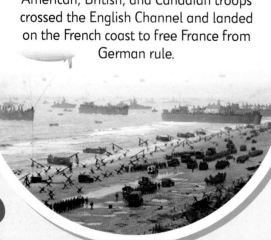

The Holocaust

The Nazis killed Jewish people just because they were Jewish. During the Holocaust, Jews were sent to camps to be killed. More than six million died.

Axis countries
Germany, Italy, and Japan formed a group in 1940.

The Allies
Britain, France, Russia, and the US teamed up.

Neutrals
Some countries didn't fight on either side.

Battle sites
Brave fighting took place on far-apart battlefields.

SCALE

0   1000 miles
0   1000 kilometres

SOVIET UNION

JAPAN

America dropped the world's first atomic bomb on Hiroshima, Japan, in **1945**.

Hiroshima

CHINA

German troops surrounded the city of Stalingrad from **1942** to **1943** but were defeated by the Russians.

The Japanese attack on Pearl Harbor in December **1941** brought the USA into the war.

Okinawa, 1945

Iwo Jima, 1945

The Japanese suffered a major defeat at the hands of the US navy at Midway in **1942**.

Midway

Pearl Harbor

alingrad

Leyte Gulf, Philippines

America won against Japan in the largest WWII naval battle in **1944**.

PACIFIC OCEAN

Guadalcanal 1942–1943

SCALE

0   500 miles
0   500 kilometres

Coral Sea, 1942

N
W   E
S

Pearl Harbor
On 7 December 1941, Japanese planes bombed US navy ships based at Pearl Harbor, Hawaii. The attack took the US by surprise and led it to join the war on the Allies' side.

The cost of war
World War II was the deadliest war in human history. More than 38 million civilians and 22 million troops lost their lives. Another 25 million people were killed by disease and lack of food.

Soldiers' graves in France

Independent world

In 1945, most of the world's nations were colonies, which meant they were ruled by other countries. Since then, most colonies have become independent. Some countries gained their freedom peacefully, while others had to fight for it. There are now 195 independent nations in the world.

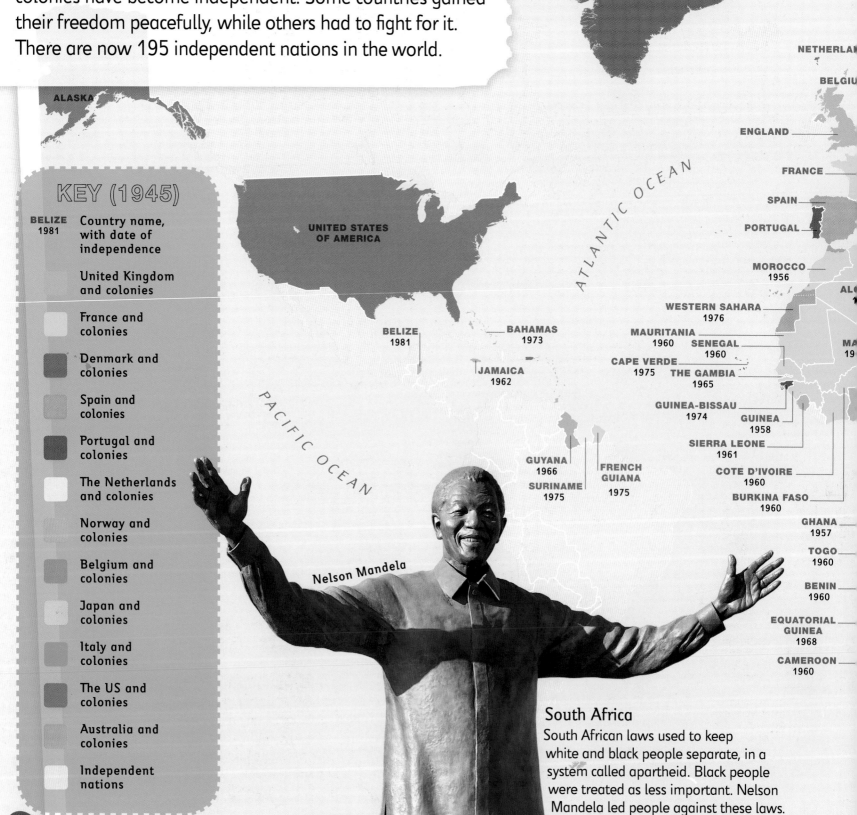

GREENLAND

ARCTI

NETHERLAN

BELGIU

ENGLAND

ALASKA

ATLANTIC OCEAN

FRANCE

SPAIN

PORTUGAL

MOROCCO
1956

AL

KEY (1945)

BELIZE 1981	Country name, with date of independence
	United Kingdom and colonies
	France and colonies
	Denmark and colonies
	Spain and colonies
	Portugal and colonies
	The Netherlands and colonies
	Norway and colonies
	Belgium and colonies
	Japan and colonies
	Italy and colonies
	The US and colonies
	Australia and colonies
	Independent nations

UNITED STATES OF AMERICA

WESTERN SAHARA
1976

BELIZE
1981

BAHAMAS
1973

MAURITANIA
1960

SENEGAL
1960

MA
19

JAMAICA
1962

CAPE VERDE
1975

THE GAMBIA
1965

PACIFIC OCEAN

GUINEA-BISSAU
1974

GUINEA
1958

SIERRA LEONE
1961

GUYANA
1966

FRENCH
GUIANA
1975

COTE D'IVOIRE
1960

SURINAME
1975

BURKINA FASO
1960

GHANA
1957

TOGO
1960

Nelson Mandela

BENIN
1960

EQUATORIAL
GUINEA
1968

CAMEROON
1960

South Africa

South African laws used to keep white and black people separate, in a system called apartheid. Black people were treated as less important. Nelson Mandela led people against these laws. Apartheid finally ended in 1991.

NORWAY

Vietnam
Vietnam became independent from France in 1954, but was divided into Northern and Southern halves with different governments. A war led the country to be united under the North's leadership in 1976.

Colonies today
Britain, New Zealand, the US, Norway, the Netherlands, France, Denmark, and Australia still have colonies. Most of these are small islands or areas with very few people. Around seven million people live in colonies today.

The French colony of French Polynesia

DENMARK

ITALY

CYPRUS
1960

TUNISIA
1956

LEBANON
1943

SYRIA
1946

JORDAN
1946

KUWAIT
1961

PAKISTAN
1947

CENTRAL
AFRICAN
REPUBLIC
1960

QATAR
1971

LIBYA
1951

UAE
1971

OMAN
YEMEN
1967

CHAD
1960

SUDAN
1956

ERITREA
1967

DJIBOUTI
1977

INDIA
1947

NORTH KOREA
1945

SOUTH KOREA
1945

JAPAN

BANGLADESH
1947

MYANMAR
1948

TAIWAN
1945

LAOS
1953

VIETNAM
1954

PHILIPPINES
1946

PACIFIC OCEAN

SOUTH
SUDAN
1956

CONGO
1960

KENYA
1963

UGANDA
1962

SOMALIA
1960

RWANDA
1962

SRI LANKA
1948

MALAYA
1957

CAMBODIA
1953

BRUNEI
1984

WEST PAPUA
1962

PAPUA
1975

BURUNDI
1962

TANZANIA
1961

MALAWI
1964

MALAYSIA
1963

INDONESIA
1949

ANGOLA
1975

MOZAMBIQUE
1964

EAST TIMOR
1975

INDIAN OCEAN

AUSTRALIA

FIJI
1970

MADAGASCAR
1960

SWAZILAND
1968

SOLOMON ISLANDS
1978

GABON
1960

LESOTHO
1966

OTSWANA
1966

ZIMBABWE
1980

DEMOCRATIC
REPUBLIC OF
CONGO
1960

ZAMBIA
1980

India gains independence
In 1947, Britain decided to give up its Indian empire. The land was split into two new countries, India and Pakistan. Jawaharlal Nehru (pictured) was the first Indian prime minister.

OUTHERN OCEAN

The Cold War

After World War II, two superpowers had different ideas about how to run the world. The communist USSR wanted everybody to be equal. The capitalist US thought it was more important for people to be free. There was a Cold War, with the US and USSR taking sides in struggles around the world between 1947 and 1991.

The Space Race

The US and USSR raced each other to get into space. The US won when Neil Armstrong became the first person on the moon in 1969.

AMERICA SALUTES FIRST MEN ON THE MOON

ARMSTRONG COLLINS ALDRIN

APOLLO XI
JULY 1969

ARCTIC OCEAN

Radar stations along the DEW, or Distance Early Warning line, would warn of a USSR bomber attack.

DEW line

NATO, or the North Atlantic Treaty Organization, was an alliance led by the US, set up in 1949.

NATO flag

NORTH AMERICA

ATLANTIC OCEAN

KEY

NATO
Countries that were part of NATO – a capitalist group led by the US.

Warsaw Pact
Communist countries that were part of the Warsaw Pact – an agreement with the USSR.

Non-NATO and Warsaw Pact
Countries that did not take part in the Cold War.

Conflicts
Foreign civil wars where the US and USSR supported different sides.

Uprisings
Revolts against governments in communist countries in Europe.

Spies
Places where spies operated.

Intercontinental ballistic missiles

Intercontinental missiles could carry nuclear warheads to destroy cities thousands of kilometres away.

Eisenhower and Khrushchev meet

In 1959 US President Eisenhower and the USSR's Secretary Khrushchev met to try and reduce the tension.

The US and the USSR almost went to war when the USSR placed nuclear weapons in Cuba in 1962.

Cuban Missile Crisis

The US funded rebels fighting the radical government of Nicaragua between 1978 and 1979.

Nicaragua revolution

PACIFIC OCEAN

The hydrogen bomb

The first nuclear bomb was created during World War II. This atomic bomb was the most powerful weapon in history. During the Cold War, both sides developed an even more destructive nuclear bomb, called the hydrogen bomb.

First hydrogen bomb test, 1952

The divided city

After World War II, the German capital of Berlin was divided in two. The western half was controlled by the US, the UK, and France, while the USSR had the eastern half. The city became the centre of the Cold War.

Berlin blockade

From *1948* to *1949*, the USSR tried to block food from getting into West Berlin. Supplies were dropped in by planes.

Berlin wall

EAST BERLIN

WEST BERLIN

In *1961*, East Berlin built a wall around the West to stop its citizens escaping there.

In *1955* the Warsaw Pact was set up as a military alliance between the USSR and six communist countries in eastern Europe.

The USSR's first intercontinental missile was launched in *1957*.

Warsaw pact

R-7 Semyorka

ASIA

The USSR tested its first nuclear bomb in *1949*.

First Lightning

In *1961*, Yuri Gagarin from the USSR became the first man in space.

Yuri Gagarin

China became a communist state in *1949*, under Mao Zedong.

Chinese civil war

An attempt by communist North Korea to take over South Korea was stopped by American-led troops between *1950* and *1953*.

Korean war

The Iron Curtain

EUROPE

The two sides of the Cold War faced each other across an "Iron Curtain" dividing Europe.

Afghan war

USSR and US soldiers helped different sides in Afghanistan between *1979* and *1989*.

Between *1964* and *1975*, US troops failed to help South Vietnam beat Communist North Vietnam.

Vietnam War

AFRICA

The end of the Cold War

In 1989, communist governments in Europe began to lose control. The Berlin Wall was pulled down in this year, and Germany was united in 1990. The USSR itself collapsed in 1991. The Cold War was over.

The US and USSR supported opposing sides in this war between *1975* and *2002*.

Angolan war

Close enemies

The US and USSR faced each other across the Arctic Circle. At their closest, there was only 3.8 kilometres (2.4 miles) between them.

The fall of the Berlin Wall

The Space Age

The first object left Earth in 1957 – a tiny spacecraft called *Sputnik*. The Space Age had begun! A human flew in space for the first time in 1961 and people walked on the Moon in 1969. People have continued to explore space, finding out more and more about what exists beyond our world.

Landing on the surface of a comet

The Rosetta mission

On 12 November 2014, a spacecraft landed on a comet for the first time. Unfortunately, it landed in the shadow of a cliff and so could not recharge its batteries, which were powered by the Sun. After two days, its power ran out and it went silent.

Man on the Moon

On 20 July 1969, American Neil Armstrong became the first person to walk on the Moon. Along with Buzz Aldrin, he spent about 150 minutes walking around and collecting rock samples.

In **1959**, the Luna 2 became the first spacecraft to reach the Moon.

Luna 2

The first-ever satellite was launched into space by Russia on 4 October **1957**. It was 58 cm (23 in) wide.

Sputnik 1

Jupiter

The Sun

Mercury

Venus

Earth

Mars

Mariner 10

The Mariner 10 travelled from Venus to Mercury between **1974** and **1975**.

Venera 9

In **1975**, Venera 9 returned photographs of the surface of Venus to Earth.

Salyut 1

The first space station was launched into space by the Russians on 19 April **1971**. It stayed there for 175 days.

Viking 2

The American Viking 2 spent 1,316 days on the surface of Mars, from **1976** to **1980**.

Pioneer 10

Pioneer 10 *became the first spacecraft to leave the Solar System, in* **1983**.

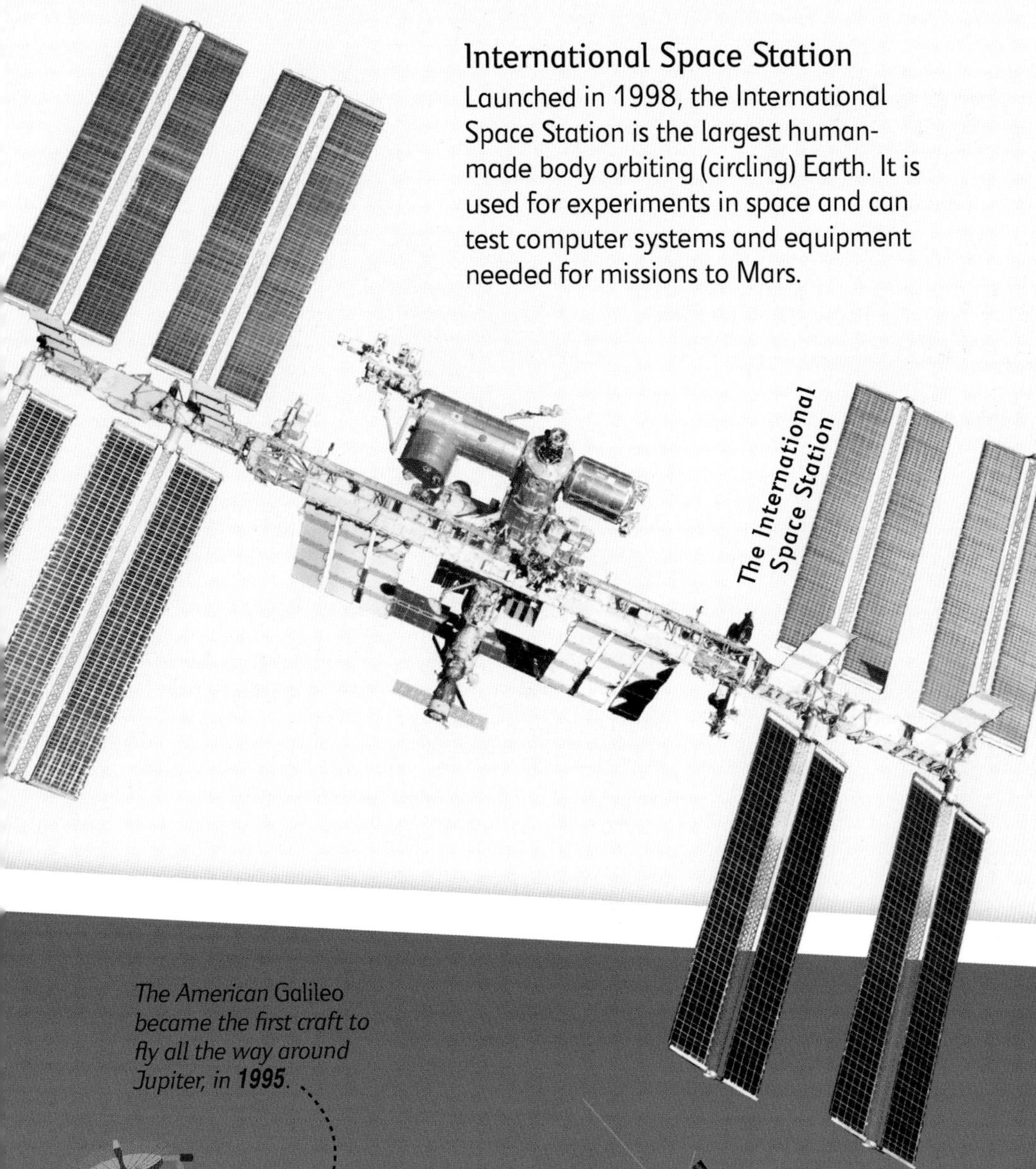

International Space Station

Launched in 1998, the International Space Station is the largest human-made body orbiting (circling) Earth. It is used for experiments in space and can test computer systems and equipment needed for missions to Mars.

The International Space Station

A satellite above Earth

Satellites

Sputnik I was the first satellite sent into space, in 1957. Today, satellites are used to pass on signals for TV programmes and telephone calls. They also gather data about weather and locations for digital maps.

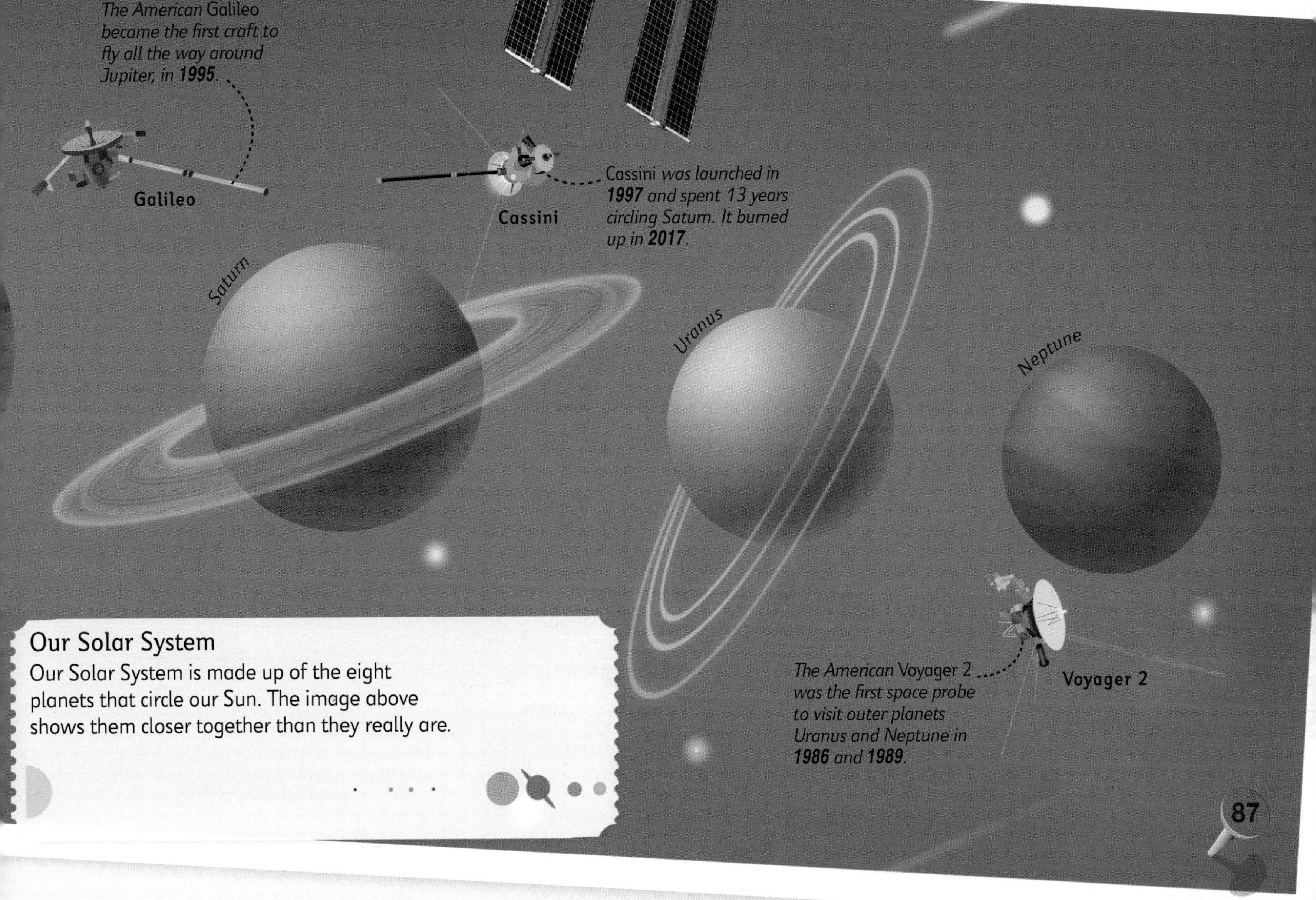

The American Galileo became the first craft to fly all the way around Jupiter, in **1995**.

Galileo

Cassini

Cassini *was launched in* **1997** *and spent 13 years circling Saturn. It burned up in* **2017**.

Saturn

Uranus

Neptune

Our Solar System

Our Solar System is made up of the eight planets that circle our Sun. The image above shows them closer together than they really are.

The American Voyager 2 was the first space probe to visit outer planets Uranus and Neptune in **1986** and **1989**.

Voyager 2

The world today

Just under eight billion people are alive in 2018, in 195 countries. That number is expected to rise to 11.2 billion by the year 2100. China is the world's most populated nation, with around 8,800 Chinese babies born every day.

Uniting the world
The United Nations (UN), set up in 1945, is an organisation that works to keep peace around the world. Almost every country today is a member of the UN.

World cities
In 2009, for the first time in history, more people lived in towns and cities than in the countryside. This is likely to continue as the world's population rises.

New York City, US

World's newest nation
New nations are still forming. The world's newest nation is South Sudan, which broke away from Sudan in 2011 after a long fight for independence.

GREENLAND (DENMARK)

ICELAND

ALASKA (UNITED STATES)

CANADA

NORTH AMERICA

UNITED STATES

HAWAII (UNITED STATES)

MEXICO
BELIZE
GUATEMALA
EL SALVADOR HONDURAS
NICARAGUA
COSTA RICA
PANAMA

BAHAMAS
HAITI
DOMINICAN REPUBLIC
PUERTO RICO
CUBA
JAMAICA
GRENADA

ST KITTS & NEVIS
ANTIGUA & BARBUDA
DOMINICA
ST LUCIA
BARBADOS
ST VINCENT &
THE GRENADINES
TRINIDAD
& TOBAGO

ALGERIA
MOROCCO
WESTERN SAHARA (DISPUTED)
MAURITANIA
SENEGAL
CAPE VERDE
THE GAMBIA
GUINEA-BISSAU
GUINEA
BURKINA FASO
SIERRA LEONE
LIBERIA
CÔTE D'IVOIRE
GHANA
TOGO
BENIN
CAMEROON
EQUATORIAL GUINEA
SÃO TOMÉ & PRÍNCIPE
GABON

MALI

VENEZUELA
COLOMBIA
GALÁPAGOS ISLANDS (ECUADOR)
ECUADOR
GUYANA
SURINAME
FRENCH GUIANA

PACIFIC OCEAN

SOUTH AMERICA

PERU
BOLIVIA
BRAZIL
PARAGUAY
CHILE
URUGUAY
ARGENTINA

ATLANTIC OCEAN

FALKLAND ISLANDS (UNITED KINGDOM)

88

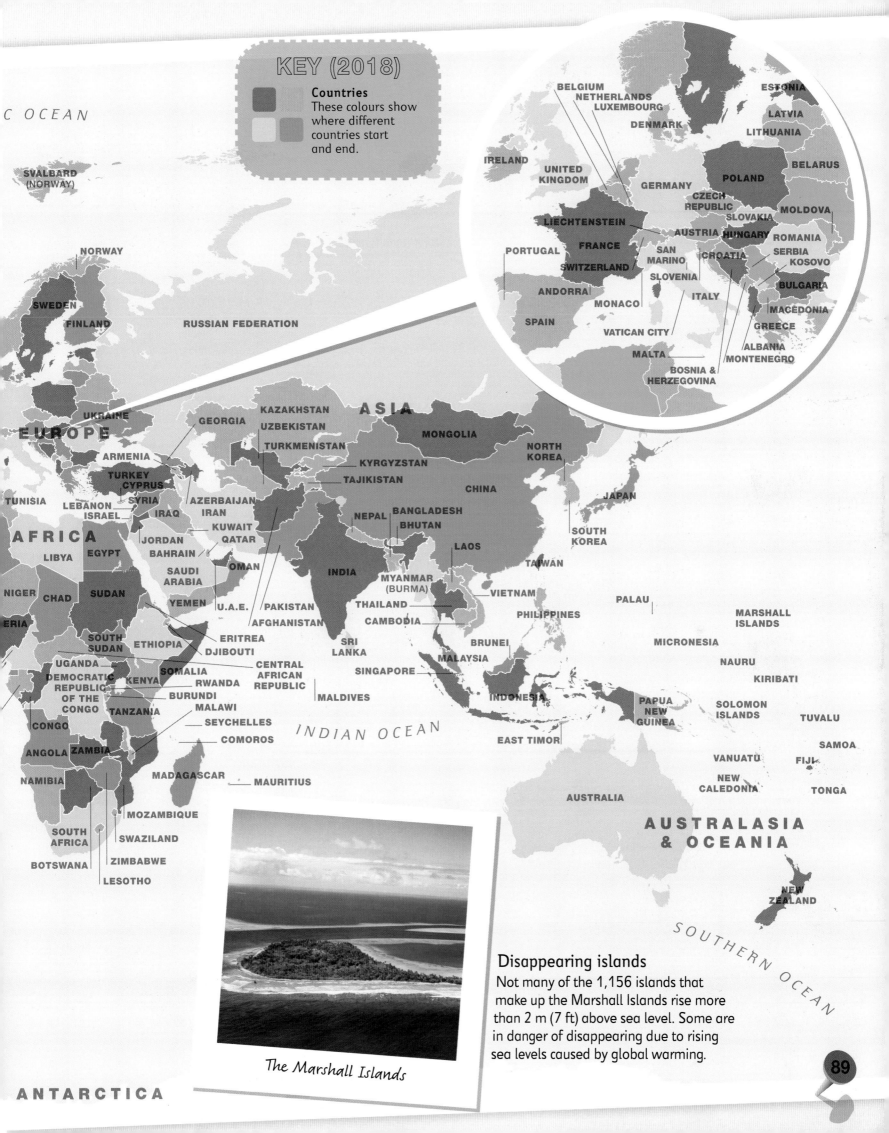

KEY (2018)

Countries
These colours show where different countries start and end.

SVALBARD
(NORWAY)

NORWAY

SWEDEN
FINLAND

RUSSIAN FEDERATION

UKRAINE

EUROPE

ARMENIA

TURKEY
CYPRUS

TUNISIA
LEBANON
ISRAEL
SYRIA
IRAQ

AFRICA

LIBYA
EGYPT

JORDAN
BAHRAIN

NIGER
CHAD
SUDAN
SAUDI
ARABIA

ERIA

YEMEN
U.A.E.

SOUTH
SUDAN
ETHIOPIA
ERITREA
DJIBOUTI

UGANDA
SOMALIA
CENTRAL
AFRICAN
REPUBLIC

DEMOCRATIC
REPUBLIC
OF THE
CONGO
KENYA
RWANDA
BURUNDI

TANZANIA
MALAWI

CONGO
SEYCHELLES

ANGOLA
ZAMBIA
COMOROS

NAMIBIA
MADAGASCAR
MAURITIUS

MOZAMBIQUE

SOUTH
AFRICA
SWAZILAND

BOTSWANA
ZIMBABWE

LESOTHO

GEORGIA
KAZAKHSTAN
ASIA
UZBEKISTAN
TURKMENISTAN
MONGOLIA
NORTH
KOREA
KYRGYZSTAN
TAJIKISTAN
CHINA
JAPAN

AZERBAIJAN
IRAN
KUWAIT
QATAR
NEPAL
BANGLADESH
BHUTAN
SOUTH
KOREA

OMAN
INDIA
MYANMAR
(BURMA)
LAOS
TAIWAN

PAKISTAN
THAILAND
VIETNAM
PALAU
MARSHALL
ISLANDS

AFGHANISTAN
CAMBODIA
PHILIPPINES

SRI
LANKA
BRUNEI
MICRONESIA

MALDIVES
SINGAPORE
MALAYSIA
NAURU
KIRIBATI

INDONESIA
PAPUA
NEW
GUINEA
SOLOMON
ISLANDS
TUVALU

EAST TIMOR
SAMOA

INDIAN OCEAN

VANUATU
FIJI

NEW
CALEDONIA
TONGA

AUSTRALIA

**AUSTRALASIA
& OCEANIA**

NEW
ZEALAND

SOUTHERN OCEAN

Magnified Europe inset
BELGIUM
NETHERLANDS
LUXEMBOURG
DENMARK
ESTONIA
LATVIA
LITHUANIA

IRELAND
UNITED
KINGDOM
GERMANY
POLAND
BELARUS

CZECH
REPUBLIC
MOLDOVA
SLOVAKIA

LIECHTENSTEIN
AUSTRIA
HUNGARY
ROMANIA

PORTUGAL
FRANCE
SAN
MARINO
CROATIA
SERBIA
KOSOVO

SWITZERLAND
SLOVENIA
BULGARIA

ANDORRA
MONACO
ITALY
MACEDONIA

SPAIN
VATICAN CITY
GREECE

MALTA
ALBANIA
MONTENEGRO

BOSNIA &
HERZEGOVINA

Disappearing islands

Not many of the 1,156 islands that make up the Marshall Islands rise more than 2 m (7 ft) above sea level. Some are in danger of disappearing due to rising sea levels caused by global warming.

The Marshall Islands

ANTARCTICA

Atlas picture quiz

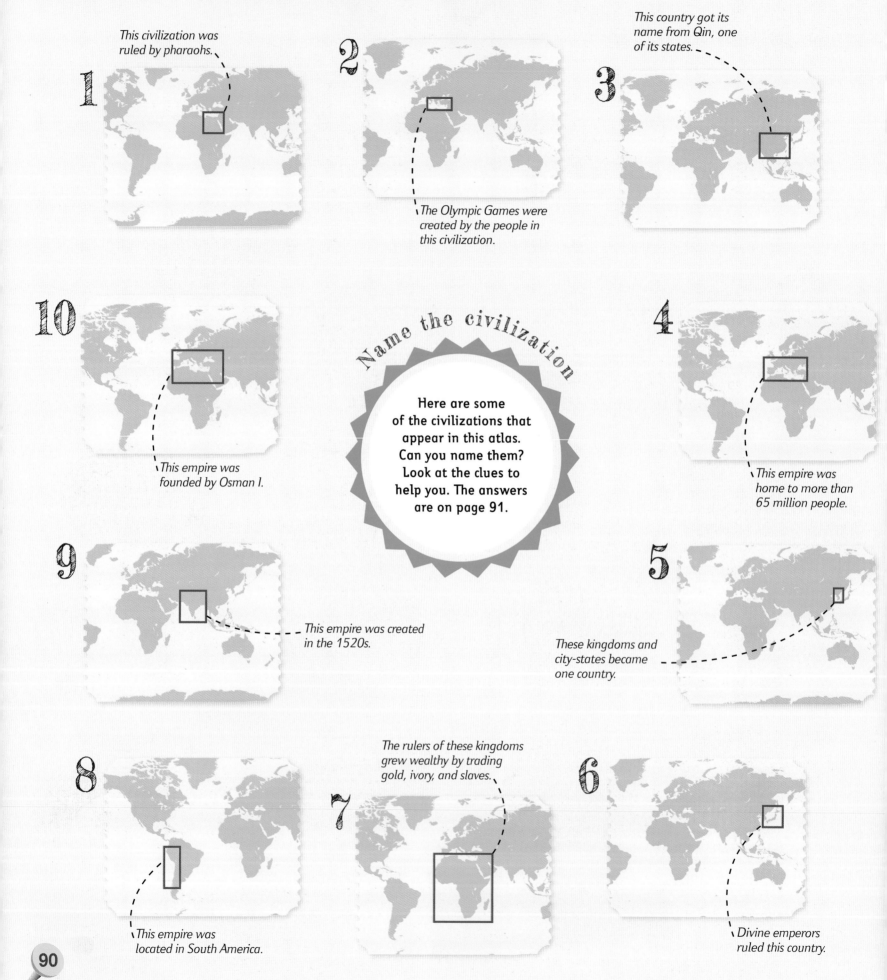

1 This civilization was ruled by pharaohs.

2 The Olympic Games were created by the people in this civilization.

3 This country got its name from Qin, one of its states.

10 This empire was founded by Osman I.

Name the civilization

Here are some of the civilizations that appear in this atlas. Can you name them? Look at the clues to help you. The answers are on page 91.

4 This empire was home to more than 65 million people.

9 This empire was created in the 1520s.

5 These kingdoms and city-states became one country.

8 This empire was located in South America.

7 The rulers of these kingdoms grew wealthy by trading gold, ivory, and slaves.

6 Divine emperors ruled this country.

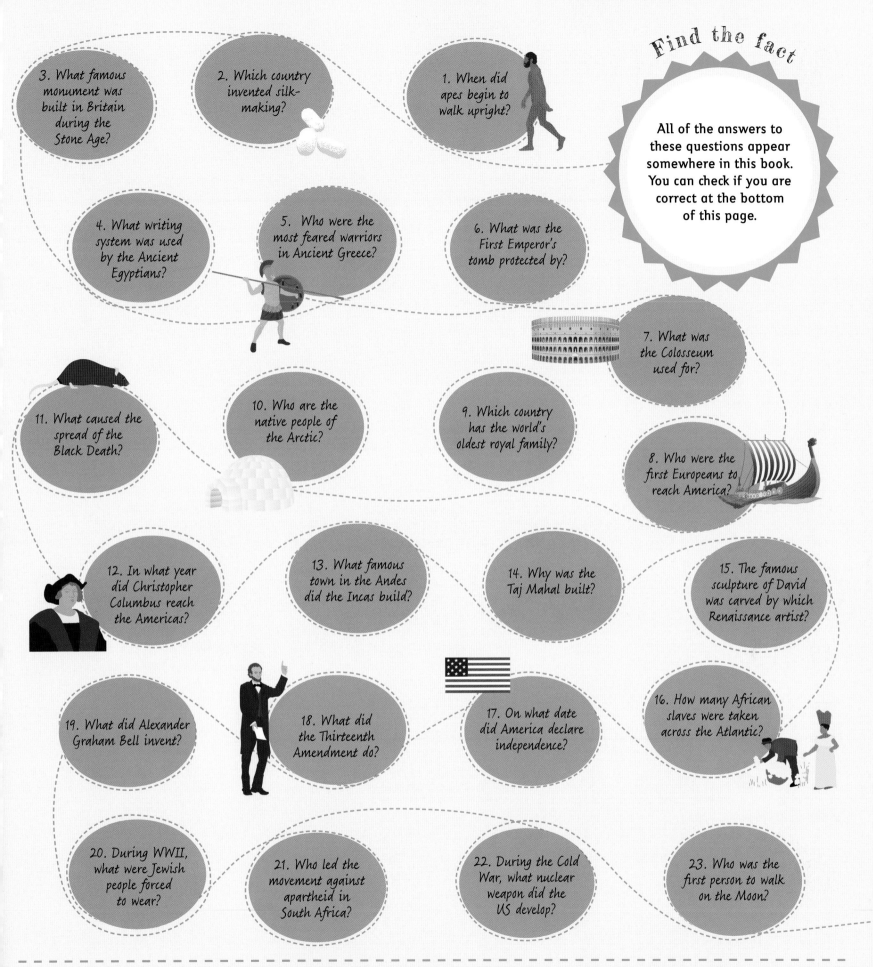

Find the fact

All of the answers to these questions appear somewhere in this book. You can check if you are correct at the bottom of this page.

1. When did apes begin to walk upright?

2. Which country invented silk-making?

3. What famous monument was built in Britain during the Stone Age?

4. What writing system was used by the Ancient Egyptians?

5. Who were the most feared warriors in Ancient Greece?

6. What was the First Emperor's tomb protected by?

7. What was the Colosseum used for?

8. Who were the first Europeans to reach America?

9. Which country has the world's oldest royal family?

10. Who are the native people of the Arctic?

11. What caused the spread of the Black Death?

12. In what year did Christopher Columbus reach the Americas?

13. What famous town in the Andes did the Incas build?

14. Why was the Taj Mahal built?

15. The famous sculpture of David was carved by which Renaissance artist?

16. How many African slaves were taken across the Atlantic?

17. On what date did America declare independence?

18. What did the Thirteenth Amendment do?

19. What did Alexander Graham Bell invent?

20. During WWII, what were Jewish people forced to wear?

21. Who led the movement against apartheid in South Africa?

22. During the Cold War, what nuclear weapon did the US develop?

23. Who was the first person to walk on the Moon?

Answers: Page 8–9 The Ancient World: 1. Jericho, 2. Valley of the Kings, 3. Nile, 4. Vercingetorix, 5. Mesopotamia, 6. The Xiongnu, 7. A wooden horse, 8. Mount Vesuvius. **Page 26–27 The Middle Ages:** 1. Buddhism, 2. Sahara, 3. Japan, 4. North America, 5. 1337, 6. The Mongols, 7. Inca Empire, 8. Black Death. **Page 42–43 The Age of Discovery:** 1. Emperor Shah Jahan, 2. Constantinople, 4. São Gabriel, 5. El Castillo, 6. India, 7. Pacat of Patenque, 8. 12 million. **Page 58 – 59 The Age of Industry:** 1. Yorktown, 2. James Hargreaves, 3. 4th July 1776, 4. Abraham Lincoln, 5. Tea, 6. Cornwall, 7. Bastille, 8. Australia. **Page 70–71 The Modern World:** 1. Ottoman Empire, 2. 1926, 3. 1939, 4. US, 5. Italy 6. 1989, 7. South Sudan. **Page 90 Name the civilization:** 1. Egyptian (pages 16–17), 2. Greek (pages 18–19), 3. Chinese (pages 20–21), 4. Roman (pages 22–23), 5. Korean (pages 32–33), 6. Japanese (pages 32–33), 7. African (pages 46–47), 8. Inca (pages 46–47), 9. Mughal (pages 50–51), 10. Ottoman (pages 52–53). **Page 91 Find the fact:** 1. Around six million years ago (page 6), 2. China (page 11), 3. Stonehenge (page 12), 4. Hieroglyphs (page 16), 5. The Spartans (page 20), 6. A terracotta army (page 20), 7. To hold gladiator fights and other sports (page 23), 8. The Vikings (page 30), 9. Japan (page 33), 10. The Inuit (page 34), 11. Rat fleas (page 41), 12. 1492 (page 45), 13. Machu Picchu (page 47), 14. The Mughal emperor, Shah Jahan, built it in memory of his favourite wife (page 51), 15. Michelangelo (page 55), 16. 12 million (page 56), 17. 4th July 1776 (page 61), 18. It abolished slavery in the United States (page 67), 19. The first telephone (page 67), 20. A yellow star with the words "Jude" written on it (page 80), 21. Nelson Mandela (page 84), 22. The hydrogen bomb (page 82), 23. Neil Armstrong (page 86).

91

Glossary

agriculture
Growing crops and raising livestock for food

ally
Country that supports another country, and might agree to trade deals or fight alongside them in a war

ancient
Very old

army
Organized group of soldiers

artefact
Human-made object, generally of historic or cultural interest, such as a painting or a vase

astronaut
Someone who is trained to travel and work in a spacecraft

BCE
Before Common Era, or all the years before year 1

beliefs
Set of views that people hold about the world, life, and the afterlife

Buddhist
Member of a religion called Buddhism, which follows the teachings of the Buddha, who lived in India about 2,500 years ago

capitalism
Political or economic system where individuals own property and companies, instead of the government owning them

CE
Common Era, or all the years after year 1

Christian
Someone who follows the religious teachings of Jesus Christ, who lived in the Middle East 2,000 years ago

civilization
Society where people have built a complex city or country

colony
Area of land or island belonging to a different country

conquer
Act of one country taking over another country

culture
Way of life and beliefs of the people of a region or country

democracy
System of government where people outside the government have a say in how the country is run, usually by voting

dictator
Ruler with total power

emperor
Ruler of an empire

empire
Large area with different peoples, ruled by a king or emperor

government
Group of people who run a country

Hindu
Member of the Indian religion Hinduism. Hindus worship many gods and believe that when people die, they are born again

holy
Something or somewhere sacred to a religion

independence
Freedom from outside control, such as when a country or area is no longer ruled by another country

Jew
Follower of the religion Judaism. Jews worship one God and their holy books are the Old Testament and the Talmud

Muslim
Someone whose religion is Islam. Muslims believe in one god, and they follow the teachings of the Prophet Muhammad

native
Person linked to a place by birth, or whose family are from the original inhabitants of an area

Nazi
Member, or follower, of the Nazi Party (National Socialists) in Germany, led by Adolf Hitler

peasant
A poor person whose way of life is dependent on farming

persecution
Bad treatment of people because of their beliefs

Renaissance
A focus on art and learning in Europe that began in the 15th century, linked to a renewed interest in the ancient cultures of Greece and Rome

revolution
Sudden change that happens when a government or ruling power is overthrown, often quickly and by force

slave
Person who is forced to work for or serve another person or family. Slaves are considered the property of their owners and forced to obey them

society
Organized group of people with a shared culture

spy
Person who gathers information in secret. In war, each side uses spies to find out the other's secrets

technology
Using scientific knowledge to create machinery and devices, such as computers

territory
Area of land that belongs to a particular country or state

trade route
Route sailed by merchant ships carrying goods from one country to another

traditional
When something has been done in the same way for a long time

tribe
Group of people who share the same culture and history. It usually refers to people who live together in traditional communities, far from cities and towns

Index

9/11 72

A

abolitionists 57
Abu Simbel 17
Afghanistan 85
Africa
  early man 6
  empires 36–37
  exploration of 45, 49, 54
  farming 11
  Ottoman Empire 52–53
  Romans 22–23
  Scramble for Africa 69
  slave trade 44, 45, 56–57, 61
Age of Discovery 42–57
Age of Industry 58–69
Ahmed I, Sultan 45
Ainu people 33
airmail 75
Akbar, Emperor 51
Akkad 10, 14
Aksum 37
Aldrin, Buzz 86
Alexander the Great 11
Allied Powers 76–77, 80–81
Alvaro, King of Kongo 37
amphitheatres 22, 23
ancient history 8–23
Andes 47
Angola 85
antibiotics 75
Apache 35
apartheid 73, 82
Appian Way 23
aqueducts 22
Arab conquests 29
Arab Revolt 77
Arab traders 57
Arabian Sea 15, 39
Arctic 34
Arkwright, Richard 61
Armstrong, Neil 84, 86
art
  cave paintings 6, 10
  Renaissance 54–55
Asia
  Silk Road 38–39
  voyages of discovery 48–49
  world religions 24–25
Assyria 14
astrolabes 54
Atahualpa, Emperor 47
Athens 19
Atlanta, capture of 67
Atlantic Ocean 30, 45, 56–57, 68
atomic bomb 81
Augustus, Emperor 22
Aurangzeb, Emperor 51
Australia 6, 60
  Green politics 79
  independence 61
  revolt 60

Austria-Hungary 68, 76–77
Axis Powers 80–81
Aztec civilization 45, 46

B

Babur, Emperor 50
Babylon 14
Baekje Kingdom 32
Baghdad 28
Baird, John Logie 73, 75
Baltic Sea 13
Bastille, Fall of the 63
Becket, Thomas 40
Bedouins 53
Belgium 63, 76
Bell, Alexander Graham 61, 75
Benin Empire 28, 36
Berlin 69, 73, 85
Berlin Wall 73, 85
Bessemer, Henry 60
Black Death 29, 41
Black Sea 18, 19, 30
Blitzkrieg 80
Blue Mosque (Istanbul) 45, 52
Bonaparte, Napoleon 60, 63
Booth, John Wilkes 67
Boston Tea Party 62
Brazil 45, 56–57
  independence 61
Bridgewater Canal 64
Britain
  Battle of Britain 80
  British Empire 60, 69
  Church of England 44
  explorers and settlers 45, 48
  Industrial Revolution 64–65
  Middle Ages 40
  Norman conquest 28
  Renaissance 54
  Romans 22
  slave trade 57
  Spanish Armada 45
  Stone Age 12
  Vikings 29, 31
  votes to leave EU 72
  World War II 80
Bronze Age 10–11
Brunel, Isambard Kingdom 65
Brunelleschi, Filippo 28, 55
Buddhism 24, 25, 32, 33, 39
Buland Darwaza (Fatehpur Sikri) 50
Bulguksa Temple (Gyeongju) 32
Bull Run, First Battle of 67

C

Cabot, John 45, 48
Cabral, Pedro 45
Caesar, Julius 22
camels 36, 39, 53
Canada 45, 60
canals 64
Canterbury 40
Caribbean 45, 48, 49, 56

carnelian 15
Carolingian Empire 29
Carthaginians 22
Cartier, Jacques 45
Caspian Sea 39
castles
  Europe 40
  Japan 33
Çatalhöyük 13
cathedrals 40
Catholic Church 45, 54, 55
cave paintings 6, 10
CDs 73, 74
Central Powers 76–77
Chang'an 29
Changping, Battle of 21
Charette, General 63
Charles IV, Emperor 41
Chavin de Huantar 11
Chichen Itza 46
child labour 65
Chimú people 47
China
  ancient 10, 20–21, 29
  Chinese Civil War 85
  Chinese Revolution 60
  communism 73, 79, 85
  Opium Wars 60
  population 88
  Silk Road 38, 39
Christianity 24, 36, 37, 39, 40
Church, division of 44, 45, 54
cities
  first 14
  Greek city-states 18
Cleopatra, Queen 23
climate change 11, 89
coal mining 64–65
Cold War 73, 84–85
colonies 82–83
Colosseum (Rome) 23
Columbus, Christopher 45, 48, 49
communism 60, 72, 73, 78, 79, 84–85
computers 73, 74
Confederates 66–67
Constantine the Great 23
Constantinople 23, 45, 52
Cook, James 60
Cooper, Martin 74
Copernicus, Nicolas 45, 54
Cortes, Hernan 45
cotton 56, 57, 64
Cousteau, Jacques 75
Crete 19
the Crusades 28
Cuban Missile Crisis 72, 84
cuneiform writing 14

D

D-Day 80
da Gama, Vasco 44, 48, 49, 51
David (Michelangelo) 45, 55

Delaware River 62
democracy 78
Denmark 12, 61
Dias, Bartolomeu 45
disease 29, 41, 64, 81
Dürer, Albrecht 55

E

Easter Island 29, 72
EEC (European Economic Community) 72
Egypt 45, 53, 69
  Ancient 10, 11, 16–17, 23
Eisenhower, Dwight D. 84
El Alamein, Battle of 80
El Castillo (Chichen Itza) 46
electric motors 61
elephants 15, 22, 50–51
Elizabeth I, Queen 45
Engels, Friedrich 60
England see Britain
Epidaurus 19
Erasmus 54
Eric the Red 30
Ethiopia 36, 69
EU (European Union) 72
Euphrates River 14
the Euro 72
Europe
  Imperial World 68–69
  Middle Ages 40–41
  Renaissance 54–55
  Roman Empire 22–23
  Stone Age 12–13
  Vikings 30–31
  World War I 76–77
  World War II 80–81
Ewuare the Great 28
Exposition Universelle 68
eyeglasses 29
Ezana, King of Axum 37

F

factories 64–65
Faraday, Michael 61
farming
  ancient 11, 12, 13, 14, 16, 21
  Incas 47
  medieval Europe 41
  North America 35
  United States 56
fascism 78
Fleming, Alexander 73, 75
flight 61, 74
Florence 28, 45, 55
flying shuttle 64
Fort Sumter, attack on 67
France
  colonies 45, 60, 68–69, 83
  French Revolution 61, 63
  Middle Ages 40
  Romans 22
  World War I 76
  World War II 80, 81

Franco, General Francisco 78
Franz Ferdinand, Prince 60, 76
Freedom Proclamation 67
Fuji, Mount 33

G

Gagarin, Yuri 85
Gallipoli 77
Gandhi, Mahatma 79
Gaya 32
Germany
  Cold War 85
  Middle Ages 40–41
  Nazi Party 73, 78
  Renaissance 54–55
  World War I 76–77
  World War II 80
Ghana
  independence 72
  Kingdom of 28, 29
Glasgow 64
global warming 89
Göbekli Tepe 13
gods and goddesses
  Aztec, Maya and Inca 46–47
  Egyptian 17
  Viking 31
  see also religions
Goguryeo Kingdom 32
Great Depression 73
Great Famine 29
Great Wall of China 21
SS Great Western 65
Great Zimbabwe 37
Greece
  Ancient 11, 18–19
  Greek War of Independence 61
Greenland 30
Gutenberg, Johannes 44
Gyeongju 32

H

Hadrian's Wall 22
Haitian revolution 60
Hammurabi, King 14
Hannibal 22
Hanseatic League 41
Hargreaves, James 64
Hatshepsut, Queen 17
Henry VIII, King 44
hieroglyphs 11, 16
Himeji castle 33
Hinduism 24, 25
Hiroshima 81
Hispaniola 45
Hitler, Adolf 73, 78, 80
Holocaust 80
Holy Roman Empire 41
homo erectus 6
homo sapiens 6
Hong Kong 60, 69
hovercraft 75

Hundred Years' War 29, 40
hunter-gatherers 10
hydrogen bomb 84

I

IBM 73, 74
Ice Age 7, 10
Iceland 30
imperialism 68–69, 90
Inca Empire 44, 47
independence movements 82–83
India
  exploration of 44, 49
  independence 73, 79, 83
  Indian Mutiny 60
  Indus Valley civilization 10, 15
  Mughal Empire 44, 50–51
Indian Ocean 38, 39
Indus Valley 10, 15
Industrial Revolution 64–65
internal combustion engines 61
International Space Station 87
Inuit 34
inventions
  Industrial Revolution 60–61
  modern 74–75
Iron Age 11
Iron Curtain 85
Ironbridge 65
Ishtar Gate (Babylon) 14
Islam 24, 29, 36
  Golden Age 28
Israel 73
Istanbul 45, 52
Italy
  fascism 78
  Renaissance 55
  Romans 22–23

JKL

Jama Masjid (Delhi) 50
Jamestown 45
Janissaries 53
Japan 60, 61
  ancient 33
  World War II 80, 81
Jericho 13
Jerusalem 24, 28
Jesus Christ 24
jet engines 75
jewellery 6, 15, 31
Jewish Revolt 23
Jews 23, 24, 80
Joan of Arc 40
Johnson, General Albert 67
Judaism 24
Jupiter 86
Jutland, Battle of 76
Kanem-Bomu Empire 36
Kanmu, Emperor 33
Kay, John 64
Kennedy, John F. 72

Khrushchev, Nikita 84
Kilby, Jack 74
Kongo 37
Korea
  ancient 29, 32
  Korean War 73, 85
Kursk, Battle of 80
Kyoto 33
Lebanon 38
Lee, General Robert E. 67
Leif Erikson 29, 30
Lenin, Vladimir 79
Leyte Gulf, Battle of 81
Liberia 69
Libya 23
Lincoln, Abraham 66, 67
Lindisfarne 31
llamas 44, 47
Louis XVI, King 63
Luddites 65
lutes 54
Luther, Martin 45, 54

M

Macedonia 11, 19
Machu Picchu 47
Magellan, Ferdinand 44, 49
Mali Empire 28, 36
mammoths 6, 11
Manchester 64
Mandela, Nelson 73, 82
Mao Zedong 73, 79, 85
maps, 15th century 48
Mars 86
Marshall Islands 89
Marx, Karl 60, 79
Masada 23
Maya civilization 28, 46
Mecca 24
Mediterranean Sea 18–19, 22–23,
  30, 38, 41
megaliths 12
Meiji Restoration 60
Mercury 86
Mesoamerica 46
Mesopotamia 10, 14
Mexico 45, 46
Michelangelo 45, 55
microchips 74
Middle Ages 26–41
Middle East
  Mesopotamian civilization 14
  Ottoman Empire 52–53
  world religions 24–25
Midway, Battle of 81
migrations 6–7
missionaries 39
mobile phones 74
Modern World 70–89
Mohenjo-Daro 15
monasteries 31
Mongol conquests 28, 41

Mongolia 20, 21
monoliths 12–13
Moon landings 73, 84, 86
Mughal Empire 44, 50–51
Muhammad, the Prophet 24, 29
mummies 47
Mumtaz Mahal 44, 51
Munmu of Silla 29
Muslim conquests 28
Mussolini, Benito 78

N

Nanak, Guru 24, 25
Napoleonic Wars 60
Nara 33
NATO 84
Nazca people 47
Nazi Party 73, 78, 80
Neanderthals 6, 7
Nehru, Jawaharlal 83
Neptune 87
Netherlands 55
New York City 72, 88
New Zealand 61
Newcastle upon Tyne 64
Newcomen, Thomas 65
Newfoundland 45
Nicaragua 84
Nigeria 11
Nile River 16–17
non-violence movement 79
Norman conquest 28
North America
  exploration of 45, 48
  indigenous people 34–35
  Mound Builders 28
  slave trade 44, 45, 56–57, 61
  Vikings 29, 30
  see also Canada; United States
Norway 29, 30
Notre Dame (Paris) 40
nuclear weapons 78, 84–85

OP

Olmecs 11, 46
Olympic Games 19
Opium War, First 60
Osman I, Sultan 52
Otto, Nikolaus 61
Ottoman Empire 44, 45, 52–53, 60, 69, 77
Pacal, King 46
Pacific Ocean 7, 49
Paiute 34
Pakistan 73, 83
Palenque 46
paper 29
Paris 40, 61, 63, 68
Parthenon (Athens) 19
Pearl Harbor 81
pearls 15
Pedro I, Emperor 61
penicillin 73, 75

Persian Empire 19, 29
Persian Gulf 14
Peru 47
Petersburg, Siege of 67
pharaohs 16
Philippines 49, 81
Philips 73, 75
pilgrimages 40
pirates 19
Pizarro, Francisco 44
plantations 56, 57
Poland 41, 81
Polo, Marco 38
Polynesian voyages 7, 29
Pompeii 23
Popes 44, 55
population 72, 88
Portugal
  slavery 45, 57
  voyages of discovery 37, 44, 48–49, 51, 54
pottery 11, 12, 13
printing 29, 44, 54
Protestantism 45, 54
Punic Wars 22
Pyramids of Giza 10, 16

R

railways 61, 64
Ramesses II, Pharaoh 17
Red Sea 38
religions 24–25
Renaissance 54–55
Revere, Paul 62
Rocket 61
Roman Empire 10, 22–23
Rome
  Ancient 22–23
  Catholic Church 55
Romulus and Remus 23
Roosevelt, Franklin 73
Rosetta spacecraft 86
Russia
  Russian Empire 69
  Russian Revolution 72, 77
  Stone Age 13
  Vikings 30, 31
  World War I 77
  see also USSR
Russo-Japanese War 61

S

Sahara Desert 29, 36
Salish people 34
Sankore Madrassa mosque (Timbuktu) 36
Sapa Inca 47
Saratoga, Battles of 62
Sargon, King 10–11
satellites 74, 75, 86, 87
Saturn 87
scuba diving 75
sea levels, rising 12, 89

seals, stone 15
Segesta 18
Serbia 76
serfs 41
Seven Years' War 60
Severn River 65
Shah Jahan, Emperor 44, 50, 51
Sherman, General William 67
Shiloh, Battle of 67
Shinto 25, 33
shipbuilding 64–65
ships
  Ancient Greek 18–19
  Arab dhows 39, 51
  cable-laying 68
  Chinese junks 39, 49
  Egyptian 16, 17
  Hanseatic 41
  Inuit kayaks 34
  Ottoman galleys 52
  Polynesian sailing canoes 7
  Roman 23, 38
  slave 56–57
  Viking longships 30–31
  voyages of discovery 48–49, 54
Sicily 18
Sikhism 24, 25
Silk Road 38–39
Silla Kingdom 32
slavery 22, 44, 45, 56–57, 60, 61, 66–67
snowshoes 35
Solar System 45, 54, 86–87
Sony 73, 75
South Africa 73, 82
South America 11, 47, 56, 61
South Sudan 88
Space Age 86–87
Space Race 84, 85
Spain
  Muslim conquests 28
  Romans 22
  Spanish Armada 45
  Spanish Civil War 72, 78
  voyages of discovery 44, 45, 48–49
Sparta 19
Sphinx 16, 69
spice trade 49, 51
Spinning Jenny 64
Sputnik 1 72, 75, 86, 87
Stalin, Joseph 79
Stalingrad, Battle of 81
steam engines 61, 64, 65
steel 60
Stephenson, George 61
Stockton to Darlington Railway 64
Stone Age 6, 12–13
Stonehenge (Britain) 12
Suleiman the Magnificent, Sultan 44, 53
Sumer 10
Sun Yatsen 60
Suriname 57
Sweden 12

T

Taj Mahal (Agra) 44, 51
Tang Dynasty 29
Taoism 25
telegraphs 68
telephones 61, 75
television 73, 75
temples
  Aztec and Maya 46
  Egyptian 17
  Greek 18, 19
  Japanese 33
  Korean 32
  Mesopotamian 14
Tenochtitlan 46
terraces 47
Terracotta Army 10, 20
Teutonic Knights 41
textiles 11, 61, 64–65
theatres, Greek 18
Tigris River 14
Timbuktu 28, 36
totem poles 34
towns, early 13, 28
trade
  early 12, 13, 14, 15, 18
  Middle Ages 31, 32, 36–37, 41
  Ottoman Empire 52–53
  Silk Road 38–39
  slaves 44, 45, 56–57
  spice 49, 51
  triangular 57
Trans-Siberian Railway 69
trench warfare 76
Trenton, Battle of 62
Trevithick, Richard 65
tribal religions 24
Troy 19
Truth, Sojourner 57
Tunisia 23
Tutankhamun 17

U

Union states 66–67
United Kingdom see Britain
United Nations 88
United States
  Civil War 60, 66–67
  Cold War 84–85
  Declaration of Independence 61, 62
  Revolution 61, 62
  space exploration 86–87
  World War II 81
Uranus 87
Uruk 10, 14
USSR
  Cold War 84–85
  collapse of 73
  foundation of 79
  space exploration 86–87
  World War II 80–81
  see also Russia

V

V2 rocket 75
Valley of the Kings 17
van Eyck, Jan 55
Venice 55
Venus 86
Vercingetorix 22
Verona 23
Versailles, Palace of 63
Vesuvius, Mount 23
Vicksburg, Battle of 66
Victoria, Queen 69
Vienna, siege of 44
Vietnam
  independence 83
  Vietnam War 72, 85
Vikings 29, 30–31
Vinland 29, 30
voyages of discovery 44–45, 489

W

Warring States period 20, 21
warriors
  Aztec 46
  Huron 35
  Mongol 41
  Mughal 50–51, 51
  Plains 35
  Samurai 33
  Viking 31
  Xiongnu 21
Warsaw Pact 84, 85
Washington, George 62
Watt, James 61, 64
Wessex 31
Whittle, Frank 75
William the Conqueror 28
women
  votes for 61
  World War I 77
world fairs 68
World War I 60, 76–77
World War II 72, 75, 80–81
Wright Brothers 61, 74
writing 11, 14, 15, 46

XYZ

Xianyang 20
Yangtze River 21
Yellow River 21
Ying Zheng, Emperor 10, 20
Yorktown, Battle of 62
Zheng He 49
ziggurats 14

Credits

Dorling Kindersley would like to thank the following people for their assistance in the preparation of this book: Caroline Hunt for proofreading and Helen Peters for the index.

Picture Credits:
The publisher would also like to thank the following for their kind permission to reproduce their photographs:

(Key: a-above; b-below/bottom; c-centre; f-far; l-left; r-right; t-top)

6 Dorling Kindersley: Dave King/National Museum of Wales (bl). Science Photo Library: S. ENTRESSANGLE/E. DAYNES (tr). **7 Alamy Stock Photo**: Image Gap (bc). Neanderthal Museum: (tl). **10 Alamy Stock Photo**: ping han (br). Dreamstime.com: Blossfeldia (db). **10-11 Dorling Kindersley**: Gary Ombler/The Combined Military Services Museum (CMSM) (c). **11 Alamy Stock Photo**: INTERFOTO (db). **Dreamstime.com**: Christian Delbert/Babar760 (br); Carlos1967 (da); Jeanne Coppens /Moramora (cra); Keith Wheatley/Kwheatley (c). **Getty Images**: De Agostini Picture Library (tc). iStockphoto.com: Aleksandr_Vorobev (crb). **12 Alamy Stock Photo**: PRISMA ARCHIVO (db). **13 Alamy Stock Photo**: Robert Hoetink (br). **Getty Images**: DEA PICTURE LIBRARY (tc); DEA/G. DAGLI ORTI (tr). **14 Alamy Stock Photo**: MuseoPics - Paul Williams (bl). **Dorling Kindersley**: Gary Ombler/The University of Aberdeen (cr). **15 Alamy Stock Photo**: JTB MEDIA CREATION, Inc. (cl); robertharding (tr). **16 Dreamstime**.com: Blossfeldia (br); Diego Elorza/Diegophoto (da). **17 Dorling Kindersley**: Alistair Duncan/Cairo Museum (br); Gary Ombler/The University of Aberdeen (tr). **18 Alamy Stock Photo**: Science History Images (br). **Dreamstime.com**: Gigavisual (db). **19 Dreamstime.com**: Sofia Katsikadi/Sofiakat17 (tl). **20 Alamy Stock Photo**: World History Archive (cl). **Dreamstime.com**: Steve Allen/Mrallen (bl). **21 Dorling Kindersley**: Gary Ombler / University of Pennsylvania Museum of Archaeology and Anthropology (cr/ coins. **Dreamstime.com**: Silvershot55 (tr). **22 Alamy Stock Photo**: A. Astes (bc); Adam Eastland (c). **24 123RF.com**: taigi (cl). **Dorling Kindersley**: Ray Moller/Powell-Cotton Museum, Kent. (br). **Dreamstime.com**: Ahmad Faizal Yahya/Afby71 (tr). **Getty Images**: Godong (tl). **25 Alamy Stock Photo**: Art Directors & TRIP (tl). **Dreamstime.com**: Woraphon Banchobdi/Pat138241 (bc). **iStockphoto.com**: aluxum (tr). **28 Dorling Kindersley**: Dave King/University Museum of Archaeology and Anthropology, Cambridge (tr). **Getty Images**: DEA / G. DAGLI ORTI (c). **29 Alamy Stock Photo**: Ian Bottle (c). **Dorling Kindersley**: Dave King/Durham University Oriental Museum (cra); Gary Ombler/Vikings of Middle England (ca/shield & axe). **Getty Images**: GraphicaArtis (db). **30 Alamy Stock Photo**: Rami Aapasuo (tr). **30-31 Dreamstime.com**: Lucian Milasan/Miluxian (bc). **31 Dorling Kindersley**: Peter Anderson/Universitets Oldsaksamling, Oslo (br/helmet); Gary Ombler/Vikings of Middle England (tr); Gary Ombler/Canterbury City Council, Museums and Galleries (tr/ring); Dave King/Museum of London (br/axe). **Getty Images**: Print

Collector (cl). **32 Alamy Stock Photo**: JeongHyeon Noh (tl); SuperStock (cl). **33 Alamy Stock Photo**: ART Collection (cl). **Dreamstime.com**: Srlee2 (br). **34 Getty Images**: Apic/RETIRED (tl); MPI/Stringer (c). **35 Alamy Stock Photo**: Granger Historical Picture Archive (bc). **36 Alamy Stock Photo**: Gavin Hellier (bc); Ian Nellist (da). **37 Alamy Stock Photo**: Chris Howes/Wild Places Photography (c). **Getty Images**: DEA/W. BUSS (t); Historical Picture Archive (cr). **38 Alamy Stock Photo**: Granger Historical Picture Archive (bc); North Wind Picture Archives (cl); imageBROKER (cb). **Dorling Kindersley**: Gary Ombler/Canterbury City Council, Museums and Galleries (bl). **39 Dorling Kindersley**: Dave King / Durham University Oriental Museum (tc). **40 Dreamstime.com**: Leonid Andronov (tr); Tupungato (cl). **iStockphoto.com**: ManuWe (bl). **41 Alamy Stock Photo**: PRISMA ARCHIVO (tr). **Getty Images**: Hulton Archive/Stringer (br). **44 Alamy Stock Photo**: Hilary Morgan (cra); PAINTING (cb). **Dorling Kindersley**: Eric Isselee/isselee (db). **Dreamstime.com**: Neophuket (bc). **45 Alamy Stock Photo**: Bruce yuanyue Bi (tc); GL Archive (br). **Dreamstime.com**: Mik3812345 (ca). **46 Dreamstime.com**: Steve Estvanik (tr). **47 Alamy Stock Photo**: World History Archive (tl). **Dorling Kindersley**: Hoa Luc (tr); Hoa Luc (cl). **48 Alamy Stock Photo**: Hirarchivum Press (bl). **49 123RF.com**: Sergey Kolesnikov (br/clove). **Alamy Stock Photo**: Lanmas (tr). **Dreamstime.com**: Albertocc311 (br/black pepper). **50 Alamy Stock Photo**: IndiaPicture (tl). **51 Alamy Stock Photo**: Dinodia Photos (br). Dreamstime.com: Neophuket (tl). **52 Getty Images**: Heritage Images (br). **53 Alamy Stock Photo**: MARKA (tr). **54 Alamy Stock Photo**: North Wind Picture Archives (cl). **Getty Images**: De Agostini/G. Cigolini/Veneranda Biblioteca Ambrosiana (bl). **55 123RF.com**: flik47 (tr); Lomet (crb). **56 Getty Images**: Henry Guttmann/Stringer (tl); Hulton Archive/Stringer (cl). **57 Alamy Stock Photo**: Pictorial Press Ltd (br). **60 Alamy Stock Photo**: World History Archive (crb). **Getty Images**: Hulton Archive/Stringer (ca). **60-61 Alamy Stock Photo**: Arco Images GmbH (c/napolean). **61 Dorling Kindersley**: Dave King/The Science Museum, London (cra); Gary Ombler/National Railway Museum, York/Science Museum Group (c); Clive Streeter/The Science Museum, London (db). **62 123RF.com**: Rolando Da Jose/annika09 (br). **63 Dreamstime.com**: Lenise Zerafa/Esinel (tl); Georgios Kollidas (db). **64 Getty Images**: Science & Society Picture Library (da). SuperStock: Iberfoto (tc). **65 Dorling Kindersley**: Dave King/The Science Museum, London (tr). iStockphoto. com: whitemay (br). **66 Alamy Stock Photo**: US National Archives (tr). **67 Getty Images**: Corbis Historical (br). **68 Alamy Stock Photo**: World History Archive (cl). **69 Dreamstime.com**: Chrisp543 (bl). **Getty Images**: Pascal Sebah/Stringer (tl). **72 123RF.com**: alessandro0770 (bl). **Dorling Kindersley**: Gary Ombler/John Pearce (tc). **Dreamstime.com**: Anusorn62 (cb). **73 Dorling Kindersley**: Ellen Howdon/Glasgow Museums/Glasgow City Council (Museums) (tl); Gary Ombler/Royal Museum of the Armed Forces and of Military History, Brussels,

Belgium (cb). **Dreamstime.com**: Gail Benson/Digitaldaisyza (bl); Oleksii Popov/Simfalex (tr). **74 Alamy Stock Photo**: ClassicStock (cl). **Getty Images**: Hoberman Collection (bl). **75 Dorling Kindersley**: Clive Streeter/The Science Museum, London (br). **76 Alamy Stock Photo**: Universal Images Group North America LLC (cb). **Getty Images**: Henry Guttmann (cl). **77 Getty Images**: Hulton Deutsch (tr); Hulton Archive/Stringer (cr). **78 Getty Images**: Hulton Archive/Stringer (br). **79 Getty Images**: Bettmann (tr); Central Press/Stringer (bl). **80 Alamy Stock Photo**: World History Archive (bl). **Dorling Kindersley**: Andy Crawford/Imperial War Museum, London/By kind permission of The Trustees of the Imperial War Museum, London (bc). **Getty Images**: Fred Morley/Stringer (cl). **81 Getty Images**: Photo 12 (br). **83 Dreamstime.com**: Hel080808 (tc). **Getty Images**: Howard Sochurek (bc). **84 Getty Images**: Blank Archives (tr); Science & Society Picture Library (br). **85 Alamy Stock Photo**: Agencja Fotograficzna Caro (br). **86 Dorling Kindersley**: NASA (cl). NASA: ESA (tr). **87 Dreamstime.com**: Andrey Armyagov (tr). NASA: (tl). **88 123RF.com**: Peter Etchells / peteretchells (br). **Dreamstime.com**: Songquan Deng (bl). **Getty Images**: Image Source / United Nations (cl). **89 Alamy Stock Photo**: Greg Vaughn (bc)

All other images © Dorling Kindersley

For further information see: www.**dkimages**.com